Based on the Canadian Language Benchmarks
(CLB 1-3)

Step Forward Canada
Language for Everyday Life

Sharon Rajabi

Jane Spigarelli

Series Director
Jayme Adelson-Goldstein

OXFORD

UNIVERSITY PRESS

OXFORD
UNIVERSITY PRESS

8 Sampson Mews, Don Mills, Ontario M3C 0H5
www.oupcanada.com

Oxford University Press is a department of the University of Oxford.
It furthers the University's objective of excellence in research, scholarship,
and education by publishing worldwide in

Oxford   New York

Auckland Cape Town Dar es Salaam Hong Kong Karachi
Kuala Lumpur Madrid Melbourne Mexico City Nairobi
New Delhi Shanghai Taipei Toronto

With offices in

Argentina Austria Brazil Chile Czech Republic France Greece
Guatemala Hungary Italy Japan Poland Portugal Singapore
South Korea Switzerland Thailand Turkey Ukraine Vietnam

Oxford is a trade mark of Oxford University Press
in the UK and in certain other countries

Published in Canada by Oxford University Press

Copyright © Oxford University Press Canada 2008

The moral rights of the author have been asserted

Database right Oxford University Press (maker)

Originally published by Oxford University Press, Great Clarendon Street, Oxford
© Oxford University press 2008.

This Edition is licensed for sale in Canada only and not for export therefrom.

Library and Archives Canada Cataloguing in Publication

Rajabi, Sharon, 1958-
Step forward Canada : language for everyday life / authored by Sharon
Rajabi ; series directed by Jayme Adelson-Goldstein – Canadian adaptation

Includes index.
Beginner level 1 for adult ESL learners.
ISBN 978-0-19-542629-8

1. English language–Textbooks for second language learners.
I. Adelson-Goldstein, Jayme II. Title.

PE1128.R3381 2007   428   C2007-905669-5

Printed in Canada
3 4 5 - 12 11 10

ACKNOWLEDGMENTS

Cover Image: © PBase.ca

Illustrations by: Silke Bachmann, p.6 (man and woman), p.43 (kitchen), p.47, p.71
(supermarket), p.114, 118; Barb Bastian, p.17, p.52; Ken Batelman, p.53, p.56, p.97,
p.109, p.128; John Batten, p.43 (two women), p.48 (top illus.), p.68, p.83 (clothes),
p.104, p.130 (split screen); Annie Bissett, p.24, p.58 (map bottom), p.73, p.145; Dan
Brown, p.5, p.101; Claudia Carlson, p.173; Gary Ciccarelli, p.2 (top and bottom
illus.), p.112; Sam and Amy Collins, p.100; Laurie Conley, p.113; Lyndall Culbertson,
p.61, p.148, p.152, p.155, p.158, p.159; Jeff Fillbach, p.12, p.31, p.34 (phone
conversation), p.70 (cartoon); Debby Fisher, p.4, p.16, p.64 (activities); Martha Gavin,
p.30, p.54, p.66, p.78, p.90; Paul Hampson, p.32, p.80, p.106, p.127, p.139 (cartoon);
Mark Hannon, p.9, p.18, p.79, p.102, p.116, p.126, p.130 (911 emergencies), p.138;
Michael Hortens, p.19, p.48 (article), p.49; Rod Hunt, p.40, p.41; Jon Keegan, p.46
(note), p.77, p.108 (OTC medicine); Uldis Klavins, p.124, p.125; Shelton Leong, p.10
(conversation), p.22 (realia), p.35, p.42, p.58, p.60 (home emergencies), p.72, p.82
(two women), p.94 (cartoon), p.103, p.140; Scott MacNeill, p.8, p.38, p.54 (locations),
p.60 (poster), p.82 (realia), p.91, p.132 (car), p.144; Kevin McCain, p.137; Karen Minot,
p.28 (family album), p.34 (calendar), p.46 (utility bills), p.59, p.83 (receipt), p.94
(menu), p.95, p.121, p.139, p.142; Derek Mueller, p.89; Tom Newsom, p.65, p.88;
Terry Paczko, p.3 (numbers and addresses), p.70 (office actions), p.71 (office actions),
p.76, p.84; Geo Parkin, p.136; Roger Penwill, p.10 (cartoon), p.15, p.27, p.44, p.51,
p.63, p.75, p.87, p.99, p.111, p.123, p.135, p.147; Karen Prichett, p.28 (people), p.29.

We would like to thank the following for their permission to reproduce photographs:
7 Copyright © Jamie Grill/Blend Images/Corbis; **12** (left to right) Inmagine:Creatas,
Stockbyte, Jupiter Images: Comstock, Index Open:Ablestock; **13** (top left)
Inmagine:Creatas; (top centre) Fogstock, LLC, (top right) Masterfile: Dana Jursey;
(bottom left) Angelo Cavelli/MaxxImages.com, (bottom centre) Dynamic Graphics,
(bottom right) Copyright © Dick Hemingway; **15** Dennis Kitchen Studios; **19** (top
left) Anthony Redpath, (top right) Photodisc/Getty Images, (bottom left) Banana
Stock, (bottom right) Stockbyte; **20** (top left) Rolf Bruderer, (top centre) Superstock:
Powerstock, (top right) Omni Photo, (bottom left) Bryan Reinhart, (bottom centre)
Ryoko Mathes, (bottom right) Punchstock: Corbis; **22** (left) Banana Stock, (centre)
Henry Westhein Photography, (right) Henry Westhein Photography; **36** (left) MIXA
Co. Ltd., (centre) Inmagine: Creatas, (right) Thinkstock; **39** Michael Goldman; **44**
(left) Scott Tysick, (centre) Punchstock: Corbis, (right) Justine Eun for OUP; **67**
Bluestone Prod.; **84** (left to right) Copyright © Christina Beamish; **108** (top) Medio
Images, (centre) Purestock, (bottom) Comstock; **115** Royalty Free Division; **120**
Stockbyte; **127** Photo Edit Inc.: Michele D. Bridwell; **130** Shelly Rotner; **134** (top to
bottom) Inmagine: Creatas, Kim Karapeles, Copyright © Guy Greiner/Masterfile,
Photodisc/Getty Images.

Text Credits:
24 Source: Adapted from "Places of Birth by Period of Immigration" from url:
*http://www12.statcan.ca/english/census01/products/analytic/companion/etoimm/tables/
canada/period.cfm;* **25** Source: adapted from "Top Countries of Birth" from url:
*http://www12.statcan.ca/english/census01/products/analytic/companion/etoimm/
tables/canada/pobtop.cfm;* **36** Source: Adapted from "Census of families by
number of children" from url: *http://www40.statcan.ca/l01/cst01/famil50a.htm;*
72 Source: Adapted from "Commuting times" from url: *http://www.statcan.ca/
Daily/English/060712/d060712b.htm;* **73** Source: Adapted from "The Transition to
Retirement, from the Statistics Canada Research Paper entitled "The transition
to retirement" When every day is Saturday, Catalogue 89-584, No 5, Released
September 2004, from url: http://www.statcan.ca/english/research/89-584-MIE/89-584-
MIE2004005.pdf*

Statistics Canada information is used with the permission of Statistics Canada.
Users are forbidden to copy this material and/or sell redisseminate the data, in
an original or modified form, for commercial purposes, without the expressed
permission of Statistics Canada. Information on the availability of the wide rate
of data from Statistics Canada can be obtained from Statistics Canada's Regional
Offices, it's World Wide Web site at http://www.statscan.ca and it's toll-free access
number 1-800-263-1136

Acknowledgement:
Many thanks to all the field testers from across Canada for
their time and passion for ESL. I am grateful to Stephanie
Kewin for her insight, Julie Wade for her ongoing support,
and the rest of the team who worked on the book.

This has been a rewarding journey for me as I hope it will be
for the field of English as a Second Language in Canada.
This book is for Pirooz.
Sharon Rajabi

An Integrated Approach

Step Forward Canada supports an integrated approach to language teaching by bringing together the Canadian Language Benchmarks[1] (CLBs), communicative competence, critical thinking and math skills, and employability skills through a variety of tasks and activities. The units' lessons reinforce language through a blend of competencies, form, and meaning to take language learning beyond classroom instruction and into the real world.

The accompanying audio CDs provide a range of listening tasks and activities that support the listening competencies.

The *Oxford Picture Dictionary Canadian Edition* is a valuable tool to help learners look up the words referred to in the activities.

Why include the Canadian Language Benchmarks?

Canadian Language Benchmarks, the backbone of second language instruction in Canada, are a complex and unique set of publications that are widely referenced in ESL curricular resources. *Step Forward Canada* is the first book of its kind to integrate the benchmarks with topic-based lessons. Each unit presents a range of CLB competencies through learner-centred communicative tasks. CLB-based instruction helps learners achieve the competencies that they need in their workplace, academic, and personal lives.

Can I use **Step Forward Canada** *and follow my program's curriculum guidelines?*

Although the curricular resources in ESL, LINC, and ELSA programs offer guidance and suggestions on how to apply the benchmarks, it still takes many hours to develop activities and tasks that would suit the benchmark levels of your class. In *Step Forward Canada*, the CLB-based units and lessons incorporate many themes and topics discussed in the ESL and LINC curricula and are ready for use in your classroom.

How can **Step Forward Canada** *help with lesson planning?*

Since the units are theme-based and the lessons are benchmarked, they are easy to incorporate into your daily planning. Furthermore, the lessons identify both traditional and non-traditional dimensions of language learning such as grammar and vocabulary, as well as communicative competence, and critical thinking and math skills to bridge the multi-faceted layers of language teaching and learning.

How can I be sure that the tasks I use address the benchmark competencies that I am focusing on?

Every unit incorporates a series of benchmark competencies applicable to the tasks that appear throughout the unit. The lessons address the competencies identified at the footers of the page.

How do I incorporate the CLBs in a multi-level class?

Through a series of six lessons, *Step Forward Canada* incorporates a multi-level approach in each unit building on CLB competencies in all four skill areas – listening, speaking, reading, and writing.

How do I know that my learners are learning the CLB competencies?

Step Forward Canada is based on learners' needs. The Can Do Checklist[2] provides learners with ongoing self-assessment and goal setting tools at each benchmark level; the checklist allows students to monitor their own progress. In addition, learners have the opportunity to practise in class and in the real world through Test Yourself, Bring it to Life, and Problem Solving scenarios in each unit.

How can **Step Forward Canada** *help me reflect as a practitioner?*

Begin by studying the Table of Contents. You will notice that by integrating the traditional and non-traditional elements of language teaching, this book will help you become aware of the multi-layered nature of language teaching and the importance of incorporating all the layers into your planning. While teaching grammar, vocabulary, and pronunciation, you will get a chance to introduce socio-cultural and strategic competence, thus empowering your learners to use the language beyond the classroom.

Step Forward Canada's *Unique Features*

- Incorporates the CLBs and Can Do Checklist throughout.
- Introduces Linguistic, Socio-cultural, Strategic, Textual, and Functional Competence in each unit to help adult learners achieve language proficiency.
- Incorporates Employability Skills (Conference Board of Canada[3]) and Critical Thinking and Math Skills.
- Test Yourself, Bring it to Life, and Problem Solving sections within units reinforce scaffolding of skills and spiralling of the benchmark competencies by providing opportunities for practising language beyond the classroom.

---

[1] Centre for Canadian Language Benchmarks, see www.language.ca
[2] Centre for Canadian Language Benchmarks, see www.language.ca

[3] Conference Board of Canada, see http://www.workfutures.bc.ca/pdfs/EmpSkills2000.pdf

Unit	Speaking CLB	Listening CLB	Reading CLB	Writing CLB
Pre-unit The First Step page 2	• Indicate problems in communication (1-I) • Provide basic personal information related to the context (1-IV)	• Identify greetings in speech (1-I) • Recognize appeals for repetition and clarification (1-I) • Identify specific literal details: numbers and letters (1-IV)	• Follow short one-sentence written instruction (1-II) • Get information from very basic short text: identify specific details (1-IV)	• Copy numbers, letters, words, short phrases to complete writing tasks (1-II)
Unit 1 In the Classroom page 4	• Provide basic personal information related to the context (1-IV) • Use and respond to a few courtesy formulas; greet someone known and not known (2-I) • Indicate communication problems in a number of ways (2-I) • Give a basic description (2-IV) • Provide expanded basic personal information appropriate to the context (2-IV)	• Follow simple instructions (1-II) • Identify specific literal details: a few key words (1-IV) • Recognize appeals for repetition and clarification (2-I) • Identify basic courtesy formulas and introductions (2-I) • Identify specific literal details: key words & short expressions in a dialogue (2-IV)	• Follow short one-sentence written instruction (1-II) • Use simplified, short, common forms (1-III) • Get information from very basic short text: identify specific details (1-IV) • Demonstrate understanding of an expanded range of short greetings and other goodwill written texts (2-I) • Get information from very basic short texts (2-IV)	• Fill out simple forms (1-III) • Describe a personal situation by completing a short guided text about self (1-IV) • Describe personal situation by completing short guided texts or by answering simple questions in writing (2-IV)
Unit 2 My Classmates Page 16	• Inquire about and state time (1-III) • Provide basic personal information related to the context (1-IV) • Give a basic description (2-IV) • Provide expanded basic personal information appropriate to the context (2-IV) • Talk about feelings (3-IV)	• Identify specific literal details: numbers, a few key words, and short expressions (1-IV) • Identify specific literal details: numbers, time reference, key words and short expressions in a dialogue (2-IV) • Get the gist, key information, and important factual details in a story about a situation (3-IV)	• Get information from very basic short texts: identify specific details (1-IV) • Understand simplified maps and diagrams (2-III) • Identify main idea and specific details from short text (2-IV) • Find information in formatted texts: tables (3-III)	• Fill out simple forms (1-III) • Describe personal situation by completing a short guided text about self and family (1-IV) • Fill out simple forms (2-III) • Describe personal information by completing short guided texts or by answering simple questions in writing (2-IV)
Unit 3 Family and Friends Page 28	• Provide expanded basic personal information appropriate to the context (2-IV) • Give basic description (2-IV) • Ask for, offer, and accept assistance (3-III) • Describe briefly a person (3-IV)	• Identify specific literal details; a few key words and short expressions (1-IV) • Identify specific literal details: numbers, time reference, key words and short expressions in a dialogue (2-IV) • Identify expressions used to ask for, offer, and accept assistance (3-III) • Get important factual details in a story about a description of a person or a situation (3-IV)	• Get information from very basic short texts: identify specific details (1-IV) • Get information from very basic short texts (2-IV) • Get key information and important detail of simple explicit one- to two-paragraph texts (3-IV) • Find information in formatted texts: tables, graphs (3,4-III)	• Describe personal situation by completing a short guided text about self and family (1-IV) • Fill out simple forms (2-III) • Describe personal situation by completing short guided texts (2-IV) • Describe a situation (3-IV)

The numbers in parentheses identify the Canadian Language Benchmark (CLB) levels

Vocabulary	Grammar/ Pronunciation	Communicative Competence	Employability Skills (Conference Board of Canada)	Critical Thinking & Math Concepts
• Names • Numbers	**Grammar** • Imperatives	**Strategic** • Repeating • Spelling		• Read, write, and identify numbers 1-100 • Identify and read phone numbers
• Classroom directions • Classroom items • Items on a form • Social conversation	**Grammar** • Singular and plural forms • Statements with *be* • Subject pronouns • Negative with *be* • Contractions with *be* Who and what **Pronunciation** • Contraction of *is* and *am*	**Socio-cultural** • Appropriate social interactions **Strategic** • Repeating • Paraphrasing **Linguistic** • Grammar/vocabulary	**Be Adaptable** • Be innovative and resourceful: identify and suggest alternative ways to achieve goals and get the job done	• Differentiate between elements of personal information: telling, spelling, printing, and signing; phone numbers, postal codes, and other numbers • Identify effective language-learning habits • Analyse personal language-learning goals **Problem Solving** • Respond appropriately to greetings and introductions
• Times • Days, months, years, and dates • Colours • Items on a form • Feelings • Marital titles • Population and immigration terms	**Grammar** • Information questions with *be* • *Yes/No* questions with *be*	**Socio-cultural** • Understanding the appropriateness of asking for help **Functional** • Requesting assistance **Linguistic** • Grammar/vocabulary	**Use Numbers** • Decide what needs to be measured or calculated **Think & Solve Problems** • Assess situations and identify problems	• Interpret clock times and dates • Interpret a calendar • Analyse population statistics • Interpret graphs **Real-life Math** • Synthesize information to create a graph **Problem Solving** • Determine how to solve problems and ask for help in the classroom
• Family members • Eye colour • Hair colour • Other physical descriptions • Ordinal numbers • Percentages	**Grammar** • *A* or *an* • Possessives • Questions and answers with possessives • Connected discourse *(but)* **Pronunciation** • Consonant cluster *st, nd, rd, th*	**Socio-cultural** • Social & cultural conventions about birthdays and other important days • Cultural interpretations of family sizes in North America **Linguistic** • Grammar/vocabulary	**Communicate** • Read and understand information presented in a variety of forms (e.g., graphs) **Think & Solve Problems** • Implement solutions	• Identify dates • Recognize and associate ordinal numbers with dates • Compare family sizes • Interpret information in a chart • Recognize percentages **Real-life Math** • Calculate days between events **Problem Solving** • Find and correct an error on a document

Vocabulary	Grammar/Pronunciation	Communicative Competence	Employability Skills (Conference Board of Canada)	Critical Thinking & Math Concepts
• Rooms and other areas in the home • Furniture and appliances • Things to do at home • Items on a bill • Items on an envelope	**Grammar** • *This* and *that* • The present continuous • Present continuous using *Yes/no* questions • Subject and object pronouns • Connected discourse *(and)*	**Socio-cultural** • Customs and conventions in shared housing (paying bills) • Attitudes towards conservation **Functional** • Requesting assistance in writing notes **Linguistic** • Linguistic • Grammar/vocabulary	**Communicate** • Read and understand information presented in a variety of forms (e.g., charts) • Speak so others pay attention and understand **Use Numbers** • Make estimates and verify calculations **Think & Solve Problems** • Assess situations and identify problems • Be creative and innovative in exploring possible solutions	• Describe objects in rooms • Analyse personal activity items • Decide when to pay bills **Real-life Math** • Add utility bill totals **Problem Solving** • Delegate responsibility
• Places in a neighbourhood • Things in a neighbourhood • Descriptions of locations • Directions • Emergencies	**Grammar** • Prepositions of location • *There is* and *there are* • Questions and answers with *there is* and *there are* • *How many* **Pronunciation** • Word/sentence stress	**Strategic** • Attitude and approach to overcoming communication breakdown **Textual** • Coherent and cohesive sentence connection **Functional** • Convey communicative intent when asking for help **Linguistic** • Grammar/vocabulary	**Communicate** • Read and understand information presented in a variety of forms (e.g., graphs, maps, diagrams) **Use Numbers** • Make estimates and verify calculations **Think & Solve Problems** • Assess situations and identify problems	• Interpret information from a map • Label a map • Ask for and give directions • Make an emergency exit map **Real-life Math** • Determine distance between points on a map **Problem Solving** • Determine what to do when lost
• Everyday activities • Ways to relax • Office machines and equipment • Housework	**Grammar** • The simple present • Contractions of *do* • Questions and answers using the simple present • *Have a little* or *a lot* **Pronunciation** • "s", "z", & "iz" sounds	**Socio-cultural** • Conventions about politeness • Sensitivity to register **Functional** • Convey communicative intent to get the job done **Linguistic** • Grammar/vocabulary	**Communicate** • Read and understand information presented in a variety of forms (e.g., words) • Listen and ask questions to understand and appreciate others' points of view **Demonstrate Positive Attitudes & Behaviours** • Deal with people, problems, and situations with honesty, integrity, and personal ethics **Think & Solve Problems** • Evaluate solutions to make recommendations or decisions	• Differentiate between daily and special activities • Analyse problems and ask for help with an office machine • Estimate duration of various activities **Problem Solving** • Determine how to solve problems and ask for help in the workplace

Vocabulary	Grammar/ Pronunciation	Communicative Competence	Employability Skills (Conference Board of Canada)	Critical Thinking & Math Concepts
• Money and methods of payment • Clothing • Shopping • Clothing sizes and prices • ATMs and banking	**Grammar** • *How much/how many* with the simple present • The simple present with *have, want,* and *need* • Simple present *Yes/No* questions • *A, some,* and *any* **Pronunciation** • Syllable Stress	**Functional** • Communicative intent (exchange of information and social interaction between customer and salesperson) **Linguistic** • Grammar/ vocabulary	**Communicate** • Read and understand information presented in a variety of forms • Write and speak so others pay attention and understand **Use Numbers** • Make estimates and verify calculations **Think & Solve Problems** • Assess situations and identify problems • Be creative and innovative in exploring possible solutions	• Calculate totals of money and personal cheques • Examine values of coins and bills • Compare and contrast clothing **Real-life Math** • Calculate amounts of change when paying for items **Problem Solving** • Resolve ATM problems
• Food • Food shopping • Ordering food • Nutrition and eating habits	**Grammar** • Frequency expressions • How often Adverbs of frequency **Pronunciation** • Rising and falling intonation	**Socio-cultural** • Culture of eating out/ordering in • Fast food culture **Strategic** • Coping with communication breakdown when ordering food **Linguistic** • Grammar/ vocabulary	**Communicate** • Read and understand information presented in a variety of forms (e.g., words, charts, diagrams) • Write and speak so others pay attention and understand • Listen and ask questions to understand and appreciate the points of view of others **Use Numbers** • Decide what needs to be measured or calculated **Think & Solve Problems** • Assess situations and identify problems • Seek different points of view and evaluate them based on facts • Recognize the human and interpersonal dimensions of a problem	• Interpret items on a menu • Analyse healthy and unhealthy eating habits **Real-life Math** • Calculate the total of a bill **Problem Solving** • Analyse and negotiate good eating habits for family members
• Parts of the body • Illness and injury • Medical instructions and advice • Items on an appointment card • Preventive care	**Grammar** • *Have to* • Questions and answers with *have to* • *On* or *at* • Irregular plurals **Pronunciation** • Reduction in *have to* and *has to*	**Socio-cultural** • Cultural references to making and negotiating medical appointments **Linguistic** • Grammar/ vocabulary	**Communicate** • Read and understand information presented in a variety of forms • Listen and ask questions to understand and appreciate the points of view of others **Demonstrate Positive Attitudes & Behaviours** • Deal with people, problems, and situations with honesty, integrity, and personal ethics • Take care of your personal health **Think & Solve Problems** • Evaluate solutions to make recommendations or decisions	• Analyse and compare medical advice • Prioritize obligations by level of importance • Interpret a schedule to make appointments • Interpret warnings on medicine labels **Problem Solving** • Determine how to handle obligations when sick

Unit	Speaking CLB	Listening CLB	Reading CLB	Writing CLB
Unit 10 Getting the Job Page 112	• Provide expanded basic personal information appropriate to the context (2-IV) • Ask and grant permission (3-III) • Tell a story about personal experience (3-IV) • Describe briefly a person, object, situation, and daily routine (3-IV) • Express immediate and future needs, wants, and plans (3-IV) • Relate a story about an everyday activity (4-IV)	• Identify specific details: words and short expressions in a dialogue (2-IV) • Identify expressions used to ask and grant permission (3-III) • Get the gist, key information, and important factual details in a story about a personal experience or a situation (3-IV) • Demonstrate comprehension of mostly factual details and some inferred meanings in a story about obtaining goods or services (4-IV)	• Understand very short basic common forms (2-III) • Identify main idea and specific details of texts (2-IV) • Follow one- to five-step common everyday instructional texts (3-II) • Find information in formatted texts: forms, tables (3-III) • Get the gist, key information, and important detail of simple explicit one- to two-paragraph texts (3-IV) • Get the gist, key information and important detail of simple explicit two- to three-paragraph texts (4-IV)	• Copy words to complete short writing tasks (1-II) • Describe personal situation by answering simple questions in writing (2-IV) • Describe a person, a situation (3-IV)
Unit 11 Safety First Page 124	• Express and respond to caution and warning (2-III) • Provide expanded basic personal information appropriate to the context (2-IV) • Give a basic description (2-IV) • Ask for, offer, and accept assistance (3-III) • Describe briefly a person, a situation (3-IV) • Express immediate and future needs, wants, plans (3-IV) • Relate a story about an everyday activity (4-IV)	• Identify a range of expressions used to express warnings (2-III) • Identify specific details: key words and short expressions in a dialogue (2-IV) • Identify expressions used to ask for, offer, and accept assistance (3-III) • Get the gist, key information, and important factual details in a story about a personal experience; a situation or a scene (3-IV) • Demonstrate comprehension of mostly factual details and some inferred meanings in a story about a report or a forecast; a news item (4-IV)	• Understand very short basic common forms, simplified tables (2-III) • Get information from very basic short texts (2-IV) • Get the gist, key information, and important detail of simple explicit texts (3-IV) • Find information in formatted texts: forms, tables, schedules, directories (4-III) • Get the gist, key information, and important detail of simple explicit two- to three-paragraph texts (4-IV)	• Describe personal situation by completing short guided texts or by answering simple questions in writing (2-IV) • Convey a personal message in an informal written note (3-I) • Describe a situation, event (3-IV) • Convey personal messages in an informal or formal personal short letter or note to express regret and apologies (4-I)
Unit 12 Free Time Page 136	• Express and respond to a number of requests (2-III) • Provide expanded personal information appropriate to the context (2-IV) • Express immediate and future needs, wants, and plans (3-IV) • Tell a story about personal experience (3-IV) • Relate a story about an everyday activity (4-IV)	• Identify specific literal details: a few key words and short expressions (1-IV) • Identify a range of expressions to express and respond to requests (2-III) • Identify specific literal details: key words and short expressions in a dialogue (2-IV) • Get the gist, key information, and important factual details in a story about a personal experience (3-IV)	• Get information from very basic short texts: identify specific details (1-IV) • Understand very short basic common forms, tables, schedules (2-III) • Identify main idea and specific details of texts (2-IV) • Find information in formatted text: forms, tables, schedules, directories (3-III) • Get key information and important details of simple explicit texts (3-IV) • Use standard reference texts: dictionaries, maps and diagrams, graphs (4-IV)	• Describe a situation by completing a simple guided text (1-IV) • Describe a situation by completing a short guided text or by answering simple questions in writing (2-IV) • Describe a situation (3-IV)

Vocabulary	Grammar/ Pronunciation	Communicative Competence	Employability Skills (Conference Board of Canada)	Critical Thinking & Math Concepts
• Job titles • Items in a help-wanted ad • Items on a job application • Job relationships • Items on a time card	• The simple past with *be* • *Yes/No* questions with simple past • *And/too* and *but* • *Can* and *can't* **Pronunciation** • Pronunciation of *can* and *can't*	**Socio-cultural** • Social and cultural understandings of North-American job market • Sensitivity to register **Linguistic** • Grammar/ vocabulary	**Communicate** • Write and speak so others pay attention and understand • Listen and ask questions to understand and appreciate the points of view of others **Use Numbers** • Decide what needs to be measured or calculated • Make estimates and verify calculations **Think & Solve Problems** • Assess situations and identify problems • Evaluate solutions to make recommendations or decisions **Demonstrate Positive Attitudes & Behaviours** • Feel good about yourself and be confident	• Interpret help-wanted ads • Analyse and describe personal work experience • Interpret a time card • Describe ability or lack of ability **Real-life Math** • Calculate pay based on time card information **Problem Solving** • Compare jobs based on salary and hours
• Traffic signals • Workplace safety equipment • Emergencies • Road safety	• *Should* and *shouldn't* • Adverbs of frequency • Information questions with *should* • *Yes/No* questions with *should* **Pronunciation** • Pronunciation of *should* and *shouldn't* • Rising and falling intonation	**Socio-cultural** • Appropriate behaviour following an accident • Cultural interpretations of safe and dangerous behaviour **Linguistic** • Grammar/ vocabulary	**Communicate** • Read and understand information presented in a variety of forms (e.g., words, charts, diagrams) **Use Numbers** • Decide what needs to be measured or calculated **Think & Solve Problems** • Seek different points of view and evaluate them based on facts • Recognize the human and interpersonal dimensions of a problem	• Interpret traffic signs • Classify behaviour as safe or unsafe • Classify language learning habits as positive or negative • Describe emergencies to a 911 operator • Interpret a pie chart of accident data **Real-life Math** • Calculate percentages **Problem Solving** • Determine appropriate behaviour following an accident
• Holidays • Weather • Leisure activities • Making plans • Special occasions	• The future with *be going to* • Contractions of *be going to* • Questions, answers, and statements with *be going to* **Pronunciation** • Formal and relaxed pronunciation of *going to* and *want to*	**Socio-cultural** • The hockey culture; role of sports culture in social interactions • Greeting card/ e-card culture **Functional** • Requesting information **Linguistic** • Grammar/ vocabulary	**Communicate** • Read and understand information presented in a variety of forms (e.g., charts) • Listen and ask questions to understand and appreciate the points of view of others **Use Numbers** • Make estimates and verify calculations **Think & Solve Problems** • Evaluate solutions to make recommendations or decisions	• Classify leisure activities by season • Interpret information on a bus schedule • Interpret movie ads • Interpret information from a phone book **Real-life Math** • Calculate times in order to make plans **Problem Solving** • Determine how to modify plans

Can Do Checklist

Unit	Speaking CLB	Listening CLB	Reading CLB	Writing CLB
Pre-unit The First Step page 2	• I can ask some questions (1) • I can give some information (1)	• I can understand questions (1) • I can understand information (1)	• I can read some words that I see often (1) • I can read a short sentence with the help of a picture (1)	• I can write the alphabet (1) • I can write numbers (1)
Unit 1 In the Classroom page 4	• I can give some information (1) • I can answer greetings (2) • I can ask for help (2) • I can describe things (2)	• I can understand greetings (1) • I can understand questions (1) • I can understand information (1) • I can understand more instructions: "Could you repeat that please?" (2) • I can understand parts of conversations (2)	• I can read some words that I see often (1) • I can read a short sentence with the help of a picture (1) • I can read: names, addresses, phone numbers (1) • I can read a simple text and answer questions (2)	• I can fill out a simple form (1) • I can write complete sentences about myself and my family (2)
Unit 2 My Classmates Page 16	• I can ask some questions (1) • I can give some information (1) • I can describe things (2) • I can give information (2) • I know a few words about health and feelings (3) • I can say a few simple sentences about familiar, everyday topics: my work, family, daily activities, health, the weather, etc. (3)	• I can understand questions (1) • I can understand information (1) • I can understand parts of conversations (2) • I can get the most important words in a story (3)	• I can read some words that I see often (1) • I can read a short sentence with the help of a picture (1) • I can understand simple maps, labels, and diagrams (2) • I can read a simple text and answer questions (2) • I can read words I know in a new context (3)	• I can fill out a simple form (1) • I can write a short list (1) • I can fill out a simple application form (2) • I can write complete sentences about myself and my family (2)
Unit 3 Family and Friends Page 28	• I can give information (2) • I can describe things (2) • I can talk about my family (2) • I can give basic information about familiar subjects, such as family, weather, or daily activities (3) • I can answer simple questions with single words or short sentences (3)	• I can understand information (1) • I can understand parts of conversations: numbers and letters, time, some words (2) • I can get the most important words in a story (3) • I can understand short sentences when you speak slowly (3)	• I can read some words that I see often (1) • I can read a short sentence with the help of a picture (1) • I can read a simple text and answer questions (2) • I can read and understand a short story or simple news item (3) • I can read some new words (3) • I can read words I know in a new context (3) • I can get information from charts and schedules (4)	• I can write a short list (1) • I can write complete sentences about myself and my family (2) • I can fill out a simple application form (2) • I can describe my daily routine (3)

The numbers in parentheses identify the Canadian Language Benchmark (CLB) levels

Step Forward Canada: **All you need to ensure your learners' success.
All the *Step Forward Canada* Student Books follow this format.**

LESSON 1: VOCABULARY teaches key words and phrases relevant to the unit topic, and provides conversation practice using the target vocabulary.

New vocabulary is introduced through vibrant art and high-interest listening texts.

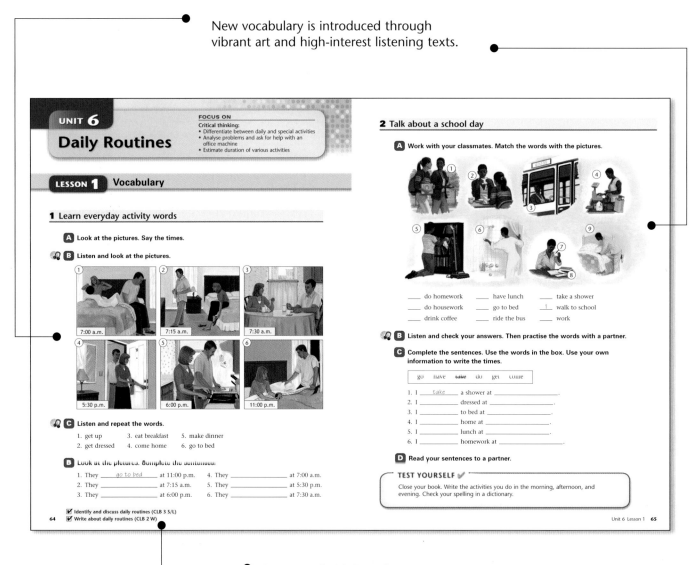

Contextualized Canadian Language Benchmark based competencies are identified at the beginning of every lesson for quick reference.

LESSON 2: LIFE STORIES expands on vocabulary learned in Lesson 1 and furthers learners' understanding through reading and writing about a life skills topic.

Life skills readings help learners practise the vocabulary in natural contexts.

Learners apply the vocabulary to their own lives by writing about their personal experiences.

LESSON 2 Life stories

1 Read about a work schedule

A Look at the pictures. Listen.

Good morning. Doctor's office.

B Listen again. Read the sentences.

1. My name is Tina Aziz. I work in a doctor's office.
2. This is my work schedule. I work from 9 a.m. to 5 p.m., Monday to Thursday.
3. I turn on the computer and photocopier at 9:00. I answer the phone all day.
4. At noon, I meet my friend. We have lunch and talk.
5. On Fridays, I don't work. I relax. I take my kids to the park.
6. I like my job and my schedule a lot, but Friday is my favourite day.

C Check your understanding. Circle a or b.

1. Tina works ____.
   a. four days a week
   b. on Saturday

2. She answers the phone ____.
   a. at 9 a.m.
   b. all day

3. Tina and her friend have lunch ____.
   a. at 11 a.m.
   b. at 12 p.m.

4. She likes her job ____.
   a. a lot
   b. a little

☑ Identify and discuss daily routines and work schedules (CLB 3 S/L/R)
☑ Write a schedule (CLB 2, 3 W)

66

---

2 Write about your schedule

A Write about your schedule. Complete the sentences.

I go to school from _____ to _____.
I study _____ at school.
On _____, I relax.
I _____.

Need help?

Ways to relax
go to the park
watch TV
listen to music
talk to friends and family
take a walk

B Read your story to a partner.

3 Talk about a work schedule

A Listen and check (✔) the activities you hear.

____ 1. mop the floor
____ 2. vacuum the rug
____ 3. answer the phone
____ 4. wash the windows
____ 5. turn on the photocopier
____ 6. help the manager

Mel at work

B Listen again. Complete Mel's work schedule.

MORNING 10 A.M.–12 P.M.	AFTERNOON 12 P.M.–3 P.M.
1. _mop the floor_	3. _____
2. _____	4. _____

C Listen and repeat.

A: I work on Saturday and Sunday. How about you?
B: I don't work.
A: I go to school from Monday to Friday. How about you?
B: I go to school on Monday and Wednesday.

D Work with a partner. Practise the conversation. Use your own information.

TEST YOURSELF ✔

Close your book. Listen to your partner's schedule for the week. Write the schedule you hear.

Unit 6 Lesson 2 67

Test Yourself, at the end of every lesson, provides learners with ongoing self-assessment.

LESSON 3: GRAMMAR provides clear, simple presentation of the target structure followed by thorough, meaningful practice of it.

Clear grammar charts and exercises help learners develop linguistic competence.

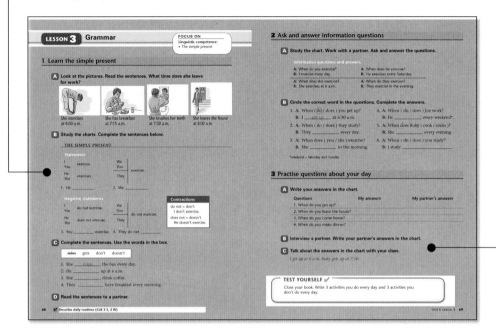

Learners work together to increase fluency and accuracy, using the grammar point to talk about themselves.

LESSON 4: EVERYDAY CONVERSATION provides learners with fluent, authentic conversations to increase familiarity with natural English.

Pronunciation activities focus on common areas of difficulty.

Listening activities build listening skills.

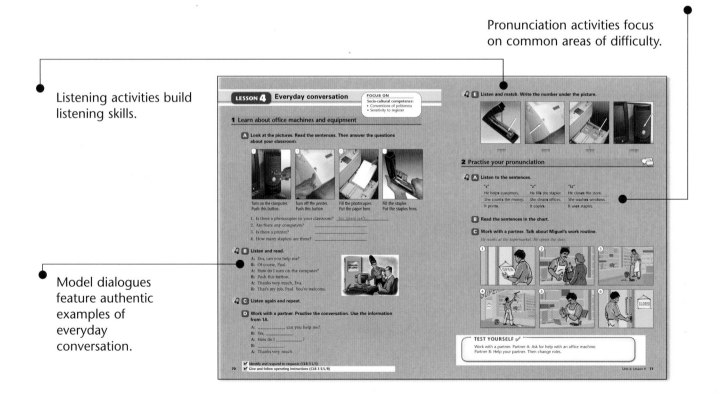

Model dialogues feature authentic examples of everyday conversation.

LESSON 5: REAL-LIFE READING develops essential reading skills and offers both life skill and pre-academic reading materials.

High-interest readings recycle vocabulary and grammar.

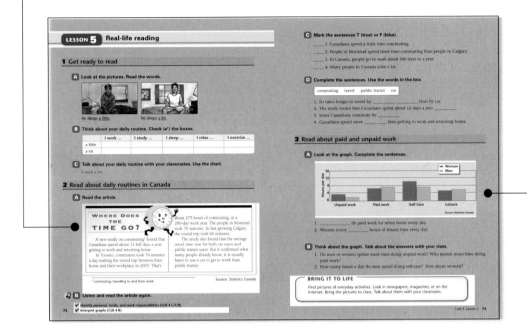

Chart literacy is increased through practice reading and understanding different types of charts.

REVIEW AND EXPAND includes additional grammar practice and communicative group tasks to ensure your learners' progress.

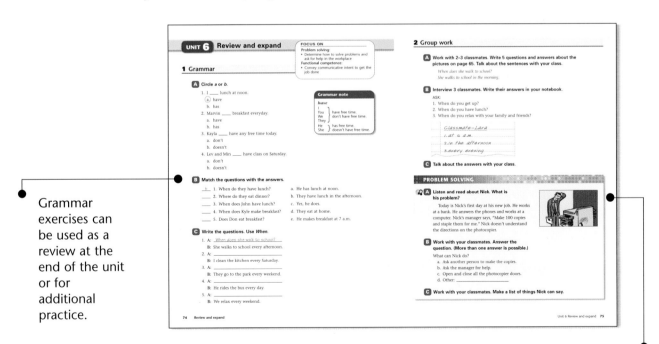

Grammar exercises can be used as a review at the end of the unit or for additional practice.

Problem solving tasks encourage learners to use critical thinking skills and meaningful discussion to find solutions to common problems.

The First Step

FOCUS ON

Critical thinking and math:
- Read, write, and identify numbers 1-100
- Identify and read phone numbers

Strategic competence:
- Repeating, spelling

Names and Numbers

1 Spell your name

A Listen and look at the pictures.

B Listen and repeat.

The Alphabet

A	B	C	D	E	F	G	H	I
a	b	c	d	e	f	g	h	i
J	K	L	M	N	O	P	Q	R
j	k	l	m	n	o	p	q	r
S	T	U	V	W	X	Y	Z
s	t	u	v	w	x	y	z

C Listen and spell the names.

1. M a r i a
2. L e __
3. T __ __
4. R __ b __ __ __ a
5. K __ m a __
6. __ a __ i __

D Work with 2–3 classmates. Say and spell your name.

A: *I'm Jack.*
B: *Please spell that.*
A: *J-A-C-K.*

A: *I'm Carmen.*
B: *Excuse me. I don't understand.*
A: *I'm Carmen. C-A-R-M-E-N.*

☑ Follow short instructions; understand short greetings and introductions (CLB 1 L/R)
☑ Respond to greetings and introductions (CLB 1 L/S)
☑ Copy letters, numbers, and addresses (CLB 1 W)

2 Learn numbers

A Listen and say the numbers.

1 one	2 two	3 three	4 four	5 five
6 six	7 seven	8 eight	9 nine	10 ten
11 eleven	12 twelve	13 thirteen	14 fourteen	15 fifteen
16 sixteen	17 seventeen	18 eighteen	19 nineteen	20 twenty

Need help?

0 = zero

You can say "O" instead of "zero" in phone numbers and addresses.

B Work with a partner. Partner A: Say a phone number. Partner B: Listen and write the phone number.

1. 555-3611
2. 555-1468
3. (905) 555-8837
4. (604) 555-9592

5-5-5-4-3-2-1

phone number

C Work with a partner. Partner A: Say an address. Partner B: Listen and write the address.

1. 1711 G Street
2. 1214 B Street
3. 613 K Street
4. 1516 Q Street

address

3 Learn more numbers

A Listen and count from 20 to 30.

20   21   22   23   24   25   26   27   28   29   30

B Listen and count by tens.

10 ten	20 twenty	30 thirty	40 forty	50 fifty
60 sixty	70 seventy	80 eighty	90 ninety	100 one hundred

C Listen and write the numbers.

1. _____
2. _____
3. _____
4. _____

In the Classroom

FOCUS ON

Critical thinking:
- Differentiate between elements of personal information
- Identify language learning habits
- Analyse language learning goals

LESSON 1 Vocabulary

1 Learn classroom directions

A Look at the pictures. Say the letters.

B Listen and look at the pictures.

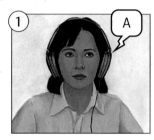 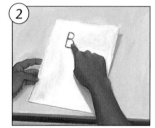  

 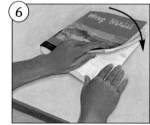  

C Listen and repeat the words.

1. listen to	3. say	5. open	7. sit down
2. point to	4. repeat	6. close	8. stand up

D Look at the pictures. Complete the sentences. Use the words in the box.

Point	Sit	Say	Close	Listen to	Stand	~~Open~~	Repeat

1. _Open_____ the notebook.
2. _____ the letter D.
3. _____ the book, please.
4. _____ to the letter B.

5. _____ down, please.
6. _____ up, please.
7. _____ the letter C.
8. _____ the letter A.

☑ Identify classroom items; follow simple classroom instructions (CLB 1 L/R)
☑ Write words relating to a classroom (CLB 1 W)

2 Talk about a classroom

A Work with your classmates. Match the words with the picture.

__1__ board	____ chairs	____ desk	____ notebooks	____ students
____ books	____ clock	____ dictionary	____ pens	____ teacher

B Listen and check your answers. Then practise the words with a partner.

C Complete the chart.

Singular	Plural
a desk	desks
a chair	
a teacher	
	boards
	notebooks

Grammar note

Singular (1)	Plural (2, 3, 4 . . .)
a pen	pens
a book	books
a student	students

D Work with a partner. Give classroom directions.

A: *Say "book."*

B: *Book.*

TEST YOURSELF ✔

Close your book. Write 3 classroom directions. Write 3 words for things or people in the classroom. Check your spelling in a dictionary.

1 Read about school forms

🎧 **A** **Look at the pictures. Listen.**

School Registration Form

Name:

1. <u>Jim</u>   <u>Santos</u>
   (first)   (last)

Address:

2. <u>75 Albert Street, Apartment 3</u>
   (street)

   <u>Ottawa</u>   <u>Ontario</u>   <u>KIP 1E3</u>
   (city)   (province)   (postal code)

Telephone:

3. <u>(613) 555-1204</u>
   (area code)

Email:

4. <u>jsantos@work.net</u>

Signature:

5. <u>Jim Santos</u>

🎧 **B** **Listen. Read the sentences.**

1. Tell me your first name. Please spell your last name.
2. Complete the form. Please print your address.
3. Write your telephone number with the area code.
   Then write your email address.
4. Sign your name on line five.
5. Please give me the form. Welcome to school.

C **Check your understanding. Match the numbers with the letters.**

<u>b</u> 1. tell   a. [J-I-M.]

___ 2. spell   b. [Jim.]

___ 3. print   c. *Jim Santos*

___ 4. sign   d. Jim Santos

☑ **Follow simple instructions to provide personal information (CLB 1 L/R)**
☑ **Provide personal information (CLB 1 S)**
☑ **Identify personal information; understand simple forms (CLB 1 R)**
☑ **Fill out simple forms about personal information (CLB 1 W)**

2 Complete a form

A Write your information on the form. Sign your name on line 3.

> **1.** Name: _____
>   (FIRST)   (LAST)
>
> **2.** Telephone: (_____) _____
>   (AREA CODE)
>
> **3.** Signature: _____

B Read your information to a partner.

3 Give personal information

A Listen and circle *a* or *b*.

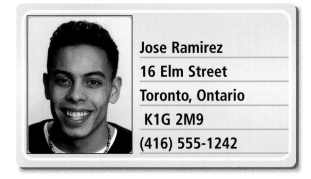

Jose Ramirez
16 Elm Street
Toronto, Ontario
K1G 2M9
(416) 555-1242

1. a. Elm Street   4. a. 16 Elm Street
   b. Ramirez   b. joseram@123.net

2. a. 555-1242   5. a. Jose
   b. 16   b. Ramirez

3. a. (416)   6. a. Toronto
   b. K1G 2M9   b. *Jose Ramirez*

B Listen and write.

1. _____   4. _____

2. _____   5. _____

3. _____   6. _____

C Listen and repeat.

A: Tell me your first name.   A: Please spell your last name.

B: Maria.   B: A-N-G-E-L-I-N-I.

D Work with a partner. Practise the conversation.
Use your own information.

TEST YOURSELF ✔

Close your book. Write your address and your phone number.

FOCUS ON

Linguistic competence:
- Singular/plural forms
- Statements with *be*
- Negative with *be*
- Contractions with *be*

1 Learn the verb *be*

A Look at the pictures. Read the sentences. Count the students in each picture.

My Class

I am a student.   He is my teacher.   She is my partner.   They are my classmates.   We are a group.   It is my classroom.

B Study the charts. Complete the sentences below.

STATEMENTS WITH *BE*

Statements					
I	am	a student.	We	are	students.
You	are		You		
He She	is		They		
It	is	my classroom.	They	are	my books.

1. I _____ a student.   2. They _____ students.

Negative statements					
I	am not	a student.	We	are not	students.
You	are not		You		
He She	is not		They		
It	is not	my classroom.	They	are not	my books.

3. He _____ a student.   4. They _____ my books.

C Work with your classmates. Talk about your classroom.

I am a student.   *They are my books.*
She is not a teacher.   *It is not my pen.*

☑ Give a basic description of the classroom (CLB 2 S/W)

2 Contractions with *be*

A Study the chart. Circle the correct words below.

Contractions		
I am = I'm	I am not = I'm not
you are = you're	you are not = you're not / you aren't
he is = he's	he is not = he's not / he isn't
she is = she's	she is not = she's not / she isn't
it is = it's	it is not = it's not / it isn't
we are = we're	we are not = we're not / we aren't
they are = they're	they are not = they're not / they aren't

1. (**I'm** / They're) a student.

2. (She's / It's) a teacher.

3. (He's / It's) a pen.

4. (He's / I'm) my partner.

5. (It isn't / They aren't) my books.

6. He (isn't / aren't) a teacher.

B Work with a partner. Talk about your classroom. Use contractions.

A: *He's a student.*
B: *They're books.*

3 Practise statements with *be*

A Read the words.

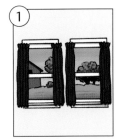
windows

a computer

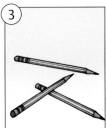
pencils

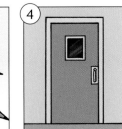
a door

a new student

a teacher

B Work with a partner. Talk about the pictures.

A: *They're windows.*
B: *It's a computer.*

TEST YOURSELF ✔

Close your book. Write 5 sentences about your classroom. Read your sentences to a partner.

FOCUS ON

Socio-cultural competence:
• Appropriate social interactions
Strategic competence:
• Repeating and paraphrasing

1 Learn how to meet new people

A Listen and read the conversations.

B Complete the conversations.

1. **A:** Hi, I'm Li. What is your name?

   B: My ___name___ is Neela.

2. **A:** It's nice to meet _____, Neela.

   B: It's nice to meet you, _____.

3. **A:** _____, Neela.

   B: Good morning, Li.

4. **A:** _____ are _____?

   B: _____, thanks. And you?

   A: Fine.

5. **A:** _____ evening, Neela.

   B: Hello, Li.

6. **A:** See you _____, Neela.

   B: _____, Li.

C Listen and read.

A: Hi, I'm Tim. What is your name?

B: My name is Asha. This is my friend Sara.

A: Can you repeat that, please?

B: Yes. I'm Asha, and this is Sara. It's nice to meet you.

A: Nice to meet you, too. Who is your teacher?

B: Ms. Simpson.

A: Oh! She's my teacher, too.

D Listen again and repeat.

☑ Respond to greetings, introductions (CLB 2 L/S)
☑ Indicate communication problems (CLB 2 L/S)
10   ☑ Understand social interactions (CLB 2 R)

E Work with a partner. Practise the conversation.
Use your own information.

A: Hi, I'm _____. What is your name?

B: My name is _____.

A: Can you repeat that, please?

B: I'm _____. It's nice to meet you, _____.

A: Nice to meet you, too. Who is your teacher?

B: _____.

A: Oh! _____ my teacher, too.

2 Practise your pronunciation

A Study the chart. Listen for the contractions.

No contraction	Contraction
What is your name?	What**'s** your name?
I am Maria.	I**'m** Maria.
Who is your teacher?	Who**'s** your teacher?

B Listen and check (✔) *no contraction* or *contraction*.

	No contraction	Contraction
1.	✔	
2.		
3.		
4.		
5.		

C Work with your classmates. Ask and answer the questions.

1. A: What's your name?

   B: My name is _____.

2. A: How are you?

   B: I'm _____.

3. A: Who's your teacher?

   B: My teacher is _____.

┌ **TEST YOURSELF** ✔ ─────────────────────────────

Work with a partner. Partner A: Say hello to your partner and say your name. Ask your partner's name. Partner B: Answer the question and say goodbye. Then change roles.

1 Get ready to read

A Look at the pictures. Read the sentences.

☐ Read English.   ☐ Go to school.   ☐ Speak English.   ☐ Ask for help.

B How do you study English? Check (✔) the boxes in 1A.

2 Read about studying English

A Read the poster.

B Listen and read the poster again.

C Circle *a* or *b*.

1. Ask your _____ for help.
   a. teacher
   b. pencil

2. _____ to English on the radio.
   a. Speak
   b. Listen

D Complete the sentences. Use the words in the box.

English	school	help	~~study~~

1. _Study_ every day.
2. Learn more _____.
3. Go to _____.
4. Ask your classmates for _____.

3 Name your goals

A Complete the form.

_____ _____ _____
(first name)   (last name)   (name of teacher)

Please check (✔)
three pictures
to complete the
sentence.

I study English
for _____.

☐ school and children   ☐ work   ☐ conversation and fun

☐ Canadian citizenship   ☐ health   ☐ money and shopping

B Work with your classmates. Count the checks (✔) for each picture.

BRING IT TO LIFE

Speak English at home or with your friends for 5 minutes today.

1 Grammar

A Circle *a* or *b*.

1. What are they?
   - a. It's a pen.
   - b. They're notebooks.
2. Who is he?
   - a. It's a window.
   - b. He's my teacher.
3. What are they?
   - a. They're desks.
   - b. She's a student.
4. Who is your friend?
   - a. He's Mark.
   - b. It's my pen.

> **Grammar note**
>
> **For people: *Who***
>
> A: Who is she?   A: Who are they?
> B: She's my teacher.   B: They're my friends.
>
> **For things: *What***
>
> A: What is it?   A: What are they?
> B: It's my book.   B: They're my books.

B Complete the chart.

Singular	Plural
a book	books
	pencils
a desk	
	windows
a teacher	

C Complete the sentences. Use the words in the box.

| I | My books | ~~Maria~~ | We |

1. _Maria_____ is a teacher.
2. _____ am a good student.
3. _____ are students.
4. _____ are open.

D Write new sentences. Use contractions.

1. We are students. _We're students._____
2. She is at work. _____
3. They are not new computers. _____
4. It is a window. _____

2 Group work

A Work with 2–3 classmates. Look at the picture on page 5.
Write 5 sentences about the picture in your notebook.
Talk about the sentences with your class.

They are pens.
It's a desk.

B Interview a partner. Write your partner's answers in your notebook.

ASK OR SAY:

1. What is your first name?
2. What is your last name?
3. Please sign your name here.

1. Daria
2. Pirvu
3. Daria Pirvu

PROBLEM SOLVING

A Listen and read. Look at the picture.
What is the problem?

Today is the first day of class at Pass Street
Adult School. The teacher is Nora Jackson.
Kumar Bannerji is a student.

B Work with your classmates. Answer the
question.

What can Kumar say to Nora Jackson?
   a. Good morning.
   b. Good evening. I'm Kumar Bannerji.
   c. See you later, Nora.

UNIT 2

My Classmates

FOCUS ON

Critical thinking:
- Interpret clocks, dates, calendars, graphs
- Analyse population statistics

LESSON 1 — Vocabulary

1 Learn the time

A Look at the pictures. Count the clocks.

B Listen and look at the pictures.

1. Good morning. — 8:00 a.m.

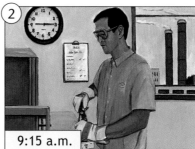

2. 9:15 a.m.

3. 12:00 p.m.

4. Good evening. — 8:30 p.m.

5. 9:45 p.m.

6. Good night. — 12:00 a.m.

C Listen and repeat the words.

1. eight o'clock
2. nine fifteen a.m.
3. noon
4. eight thirty p.m.
5. nine forty-five p.m.
6. midnight

D Match the sentences with the times.

_e_	1. It's eight o'clock in the morning.	a. 8:30 p.m.
____	2. It's midnight.	b. 9:45 p.m.
____	3. It's eight thirty in the evening.	c. 12:00 a.m.
____	4. It's nine forty-five in the evening.	d. 12:00 p.m.
____	5. It's noon.	e. 8:00 a.m.

Need help?

8:00 a.m. *or*
  8:00 in the morning

12:00 p.m. *or* noon

8:30 p.m. *or*
  8:30 in the evening

12:00 a.m. *or* midnight

☑ Interpret clock time; identify days, months, and dates (CLB 1 S/L/R)
☑ Write words relating to time and dates (CLB 1 W)

16

2 Talk about a calendar

A Work with your classmates. Match the words with the picture

Start English Class 3/8/08 ③

① **MARCH**

②						
Sunday	Monday	Tuesday	Wednesday	Thursday	Friday	Saturday
		④		1	2	3
4	5 ⑤	⑥ (6)	7 ⑦	8	9	10

⑧

January	February	March	April	May	June
July	August	September	October	November	December

____ date	_1_ month	____ tomorrow	____ year
____ day	____ today	____ week	____ yesterday

B Listen and check your answers. Then practise the words with a partner.

C Complete the chart. Use the words in the box.

Years	~~Times~~	Days	Months

Times			
5:00	Monday	January	1870
7:30	Wednesday	March	1999
12:10	Friday	September	2015

D Work with a partner. Ask and answer the questions.

1. What time is it?
2. What are the days of the week?
3. What day is today?
4. What day is tomorrow?
5. What are the months of the year?

TEST YOURSELF ✓

Close your book. Write 4 time words and 4 calendar words. Check your spelling in a dictionary.

1 Read about a student

 **A** Look at the pictures. Listen.

 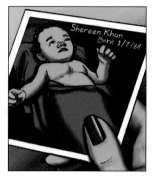  

> My favourite colour is purple.

B Listen again. Read the sentences.

1. My name is Shereen Khan.
2. I live in Vancouver.
3. I'm from Pakistan.
4. My date of birth is January 7th, 1988
5. My favourite colour is purple.
6. I'm a student at City Community College.

C Check your understanding. Circle the correct words.

1. Shereen is a ((student) / teacher).
2. She is from (Vancouver / Pakistan).
3. She lives in (Vancouver / Pakistan).
4. Shereen's favourite colour is (purple / green).

2 Write about your life

A Write your story. Complete the sentences.

My name is _____.

I live in _____.

I am from _____.

My date of birth is _____.

My favourite colour is _____.

Need help?

Colours

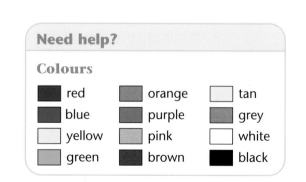

	red		orange		tan
	blue		purple		grey
	yellow		pink		white
	green		brown		black

B Read your story to a partner.

☑ Identify basic personal information (CLB 2 L/R)
☑ Respond to simple personal questions with required information (CLB 1 S/L)

3 Get to know your classmates

A Listen and number the ID cards.

First Name: Shohreh
Last Name: Niazi
Place of Birth: Iran
EAST CITY ADULT SCHOOL
Identification Card

Student Identification Card
First Name: James
Last Name: Lee
Place of Birth: China
Eastern Community College

Student Identification
First Name: Lan
Last Name: Le
Place of Birth: Vietnam
WESTERN COMMUNITY COLLEGE

Identification Card
First Name: Pedro
Last Name: Arroyo
Place of Birth: Philippines
Central University

B Listen and complete the questions.

1. What's your ___name___?
2. _____ are you from?
3. What's your _____ of birth?
4. What's your favourite _____?

> ### Grammar note
>
> **Information questions with *be***
>
> What's { your name?
>   your address?
>   your favourite colour?
> Where are you from?

C Listen and repeat.

A: What's your name?
B: My name is Tara. What's your name?
A: My name is Jun Sook. Where are you from?
B: I'm from India. Where are you from?
A: I'm from Korea.

D Work with a partner. Practise the conversation. Use your own information.

TEST YOURSELF ✔

Ask 3 classmates:

What's your name?   What's your date of birth?   What's your place of birth?

FOCUS ON
_____

Linguistic competence:
• Information questions with *be*
• *Yes/No* questions with *be*

1 Learn *Yes/No* questions and answers

A Look at the pictures. Read the questions and answers.
Then answer the question: How do *you* feel?

A: Is Trang happy?
B: Yes, he is.

A: Is Maria worried?
B: Yes, she is.

A: Is the dog hungry?
B: Yes, it is.

A: Are Raj and Padma worried?
B: No, they aren't. They're proud.

A: Is Jake happy?
B: No, he isn't. He's angry.

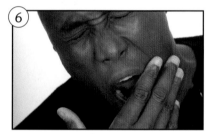

A: Is Paul angry?
B: No, he isn't. He's tired.

B Study the charts. Complete the questions and answers below.

YES/NO QUESTIONS WITH BE

Questions		
Are	you	
Is	he she it	hungry?
Are	you they	

Answers				
	I am.			I'm not.
Yes,	he is. she is. it is.	No,		he isn't. she isn't. it isn't.
	we are. they are.			we aren't. they aren't.

1. **A:** _____ she hungry?

    B: _____, she is.

2. **A:** _____ they hungry?

    B: No, they _____ .

C Look at the pictures in 1A. Ask and answer the questions.

A: *Is Trang happy?*
B: *Yes, he is.*

☑ **Talk about feelings (CLB 3 S)**
20 ☑ **Describe yourself and classmates (CLB 2 S/W)**

2 Ask and answer *Yes/No* questions

A Match the questions with the answers.

_b_ 1. Is Jake happy?   a. Yes, I am.

____ 2. Is Maria happy?   b. No, he isn't. He's angry.

____ 3. Are you a student?   c. Yes, it is.

____ 4. Are Raj and Padma angry?   d. No, she isn't. She's worried.

____ 5. Is the dog hungry?   e. No, they aren't. They're proud.

B Look at the chart. Answer the questions about Trang, Maria, and Paul.

Questions	Trang	Maria	Paul
Are you a teacher?	No	Yes	Yes
Are you from Mexico?	No	Yes	No
Are you hungry?	Yes	No	Yes

1. Is Paul a teacher? _Yes, he is._

2. Is Maria hungry? _____

3. Are Trang and Paul from Mexico? _____

4. Is Maria a teacher? _____

5. Are Trang and Paul hungry? _____

3 Practise *Yes/No* questions

A Complete the questions with your own ideas. Write your answers.

Questions	You	Classmate 1	Classmate 2
1. Are you a _____student_____?			yes
2. Are you from _____?			
3. Are you _____ today?			

B Interview 2 classmates. Write your classmates' answers in the chart.

C Talk about the answers in the chart with your class.

Rafael is a student. He's from Brazil. He's happy today.

TEST YOURSELF ✔

Close your book. Write 3 *Yes/No* questions. Ask and answer the questions with a partner.

1 Learn to talk about marital status

A Look at the pictures. Read the sentences. Then answer the questions below.

I'm single.

I'm single.

We're married.

Ms. Garcia is a single woman. She isn't married.

Mr. Moloto is a single man. He isn't married.

Mr. and Mrs. Kim are a married couple. They aren't single.

1. Are you single? _____

2. Are you married? _____

B Listen and read.

A: Can you help me with this form?
B: Sure. Write your first name here.
A: OK.
B: Are you married or single?
A: I'm married.
B: OK, Mrs. Lee. Fill in the "married" bubble.
A: Thank you.

First name:

_____

Last name:
Lee

Title: ○ Mr. ○ Ms. ○ Mrs.
Marital status: ○ married
                  ○ single
Place of birth: _China_
Phone: _(604) 555-2178_

C Listen again and repeat.

D Work with a partner. Practise the conversation. Use your own information.

A: Can you help me with this form?
B: Sure. Write your first name here.
A: OK.
B: Are you married or single?
A: I'm _____.
B: OK, _____. Fill in the _____ bubble.

Need help?

Mrs. = a married woman
Miss = a single woman
Ms. = a married or single woman

Mr. = a married or single man

☑ Provide and respond to personal information (CLB 2 L/S)

22   ☑ Complete a registration form (CLB 1 W)

🎧 **E** **Listen and write the correct title for each name.**

1. _Mrs._ Pat Tyson   4. _____ Terry Farmer
2. _____ Pat Song   5. _____ Jean Silver
3. _____ Terry Miller   6. _____ Gene Gold

2 More questions with *be*

🎧 **A** **Study the charts. Listen and repeat the questions.**

Information questions
Where is Mrs. Lee from?
What's your name?

Yes/No questions
Is she a student?
Are you a student?

Or questions
Is she married or single?
Are you married or single?

🎧 **B** **Listen and complete the missing information.**

REGISTRATION FORM

Date: _____

First name: _____   Last name: _Milovich_____

Title: ☐ Mr. ☐ Ms. ☐ Mrs.

Marital status: ☐ married ☐ single

Date of birth: _____   Place of birth: _Russia_____

Address: _3803 Elbow Dr. SW._____   Phone: _____

_____Calgary, Alberta T2S 2J9___

C **Match the questions with the answers.**

_c_ 1. What's your first name?   a. (519) 555-3954

____ 2. What's your last name?   b. 198 Second St.

____ 3. Are you married or single?   c. Pat

____ 4. What's your phone number?   d. married

____ 5. What's your address?   e. Singapore

____ 6. Where are you from?   f. Miller

TEST YOURSELF ✔

Work with a partner. Partner A: Ask the questions from 2C. Partner B: Answer the questions. Use the information on the form in 2B or your information. Then change roles.

1 Get ready to read

A Look at the pictures. Read the words.

countries

population

B Find your home country on a map. What countries are your classmates from?

2 Read about the population in Canada

A Read the article.

People in Canada: Where are they from?

The population of Canada is about 32 million people. Today, 5.4 million people in Canada are from other countries. Where are they from?

- 2,300,000 are from Europe
- 2,000,000 are from Asia
- 600,000 are from the Caribbean, and Central and South America
- 280,000 are from Africa
- 240,000 are from the U.S.

1. million = 1,000,000
2. hundred thousand = 100,000

Source: *Statistics Canada*

B Listen and read the article again.

✔ Understand and interpret simplified maps and diagrams about Canadian population and immigration (CLB 3 L/R)

✔ Write about your classmates (CLB 2 W)

C Mark the sentences T (true) or F (false).

_____ 1. 32 million people in Canada are from other countries.

_____ 2. Two million people in Canada are from Asia.

_____ 3. Two million, three hundred thousand people in Canada are from Europe.

D Complete the sentences. Use the words in the box.

| million   population   countries |

1. Many people in Canada are from other _____.

2. Two _____ people in Canada are from Asia.

3. The Canadian _____ from Africa is two hundred, eighty thousand.

3 Real-life math

A Look at the graph. What countries are people in Canada from?

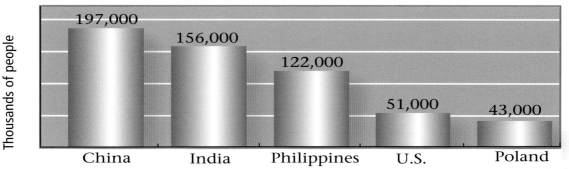

Source: *Statistics Canada*

B Work with your classmates. Make a graph about your class.

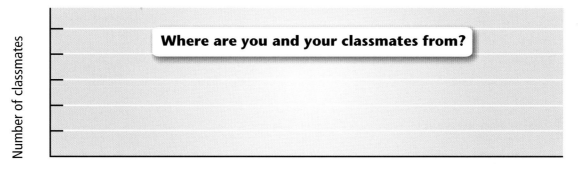

Where are you and your classmates from?

C Write sentences about your graph.

Seven students in my class are from Korea.

┌─ **BRING IT TO LIFE** ──────────────────────

Ask a person NOT in your class: What's your name? Where are you from?
Write the answers in your notebook. Talk about the answers with your classmates.

Review and expand

FOCUS ON

Socio-cultural competence:
• Cultural differences in asking for help
Problem solving:
• Determine how to solve problems and ask for help in the classroom

1 Grammar

A Circle *a* or *b*.

1. _____ she a student?
   a. Is
   b. Are

2. _____ they worried?
   a. Is
   b. Are

3. Are _____ from Japan?
   a. Li
   b. you

4. Is _____ at school today?
   a. Ms. Baker
   b. Mr. and Mrs. Jones

B Complete the questions. Use the words in the box.

What	Where	~~Who~~	Are

1. _Who_ is she?
2. _____ are you from?
3. _____ you married or single?
4. _____ is your name?

C Match the questions with the answers.

_d_ 1. Where are you from?
____ 2. What is your phone number?
____ 3. Are you married or single?
____ 4. How are you?
____ 5. Are you hungry?
____ 6. Where is the teacher from?

a. I'm married.
b. Yes, I am.
c. It's (403) 555-9134.
d. I'm from South Korea.
e. She's from Calgary.
f. I'm fine.

D Write the answers.

1. Are you a student? _Yes, I am._____
2. What is your first name? _____
3. What time is it? _____
4. Is today Monday? _____
5. What is your date of birth? _____

2 Group work

A Work with your classmates. Write 5 sentences about the calendar on page 17. Talk about the sentences with your class.

It's Tuesday.
The month is March.

B Interview 3 classmates. Write their answers in your notebook.

ASK:
1. Where are you from?
2. Are you married or single?
3. What's your favourite colour?

Classmate—Javier
1. He's from Chile.
2. He's married.
3. It's green.

C Talk about the answers with your class.

PROBLEM SOLVING

A Look at the picture. What is the problem?

B Work with your classmates. Answer the question. (More than one answer is possible.)

What can Bella do?
    a. Give the form to the teacher.
    b. Read the form to the teacher.
    c. Ask for a new form.
    d. Other: _____

Family and Friends

FOCUS ON

Critical thinking:
• Identify dates
• Recognize and associate ordinal numbers with dates
• Interpret information in a chart
• Recognize percentages

LESSON **1**   **Vocabulary**

1 Learn about family members

A Look at the pictures. Read and say the names and the dates.

B Listen and look at the pictures.

The Martinez Family

Carlos and Anita are married! 6/22/97

Carlos and baby Eric 11/15/99

It's a Girl

Anita and baby Robin 4/20/03

Carlos, Anita, Eric, and Robin 6/30/06

C Listen and repeat the words.

1. wife	3. father	5. mother	7. parents
2. husband	4. son	6. daughter	8. children*

*one child / two children

D Look at the pictures. Complete the sentences.

1. Anita is a ___wife___ and ___mother___.
2. Eric is a _____.
3. Eric and Robin are _____.
4. Carlos is a _____ and _____.
5. Carlos and Anita are _____.
6. Robin is a _____.

☑ Identify details about family members and others (CLB 1 L/R)
☑ Describe family members (CLB 1 W)

2 Talk about a family

A Work with your classmates. Number the people in Eric's family.

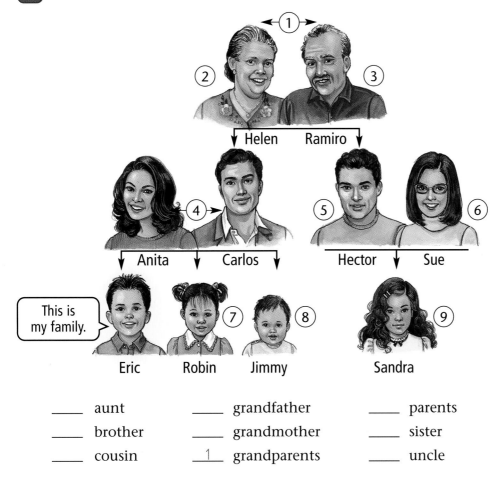

____ aunt	____ grandfather	____ parents
____ brother	____ grandmother	____ sister
____ cousin	_1_ grandparents	____ uncle

B Listen and check your answers. Then practise the words with a partner.

C Look at the picture. Complete the sentences.

1. I'm Eric's uncle. Carlos is my brother. I'm ____Hector____.
2. Eric and Jimmy are my brothers. I'm _____.
3. Anita is my aunt. Sue is my mother. I'm _____.
4. Eric is my grandson. Ramiro is my husband. I'm _____.

D Work with a partner. Tell your partner 2 things about yourself.

A: I'm a mother and an aunt. How about you?

B: I'm a grandfather and a husband.

Grammar note

a or *an*?

a father   an aunt

TEST YOURSELF ✔

Close your book. Write 10 words for family members. Write *M* (man), *W* (woman), or *B* (both) next to each. Check your spelling in a dictionary.

1 Read about a family

A **Look at the pictures. Listen.**

Sam

Karina

Simon

B **Listen again. Read the sentences.**

1. My name is Paulina Gutman. These are photos of my family.
2. Sam is my son. He is the tall boy with blond hair.
3. Karina is my daughter. She is the girl with brown hair and big blue eyes.
4. My husband is the short man with beautiful grey hair. His name is Simon.
5. They are all very special to me.

C **Check your understanding. Match the numbers with the letters.**

_d_ 1. Paulina   a. brown hair and blue eyes

____ 2. Karina   b. short with grey hair

____ 3. Simon   c. tall with blond hair

____ 4. Sam   d. blond hair and blue eyes

☑ Identify details in people (CLB 2 S/L/R)

☑ Describe family members or classmates (CLB 2 S/W)

2 Write about yourself

A Write your story. Complete the sentences.

My name is _____ .

My eyes are _____ .

My hair is _____ .

B Read your story to a partner.

3 Describe family members

A Listen to the sentences. Then complete the chart.

Names	Family members	Hair	Eyes
1. Simon	Paulina's husband	grey	brown
2.	Paulina's		
3.	Paulina's		

B Work with a partner. Talk about the pictures in 1A. Tell your partner *Point to…* .

A: Point to the thin man with grey hair.

B: Point to the attractive girl with blue eyes.

More words to describe people

attractive   young   heavy   average   thin

C Listen and repeat.

A: What colour are your eyes?   A: What colour is your hair?

B: My eyes are blue.   B: My hair is brown.

D Work with a partner. Practise the conversations. Use your own information.

TEST YOURSELF ✔

Close your book. Make a chart about 3 people you know. Write their names, hair colour, and eye colour.

FOCUS ON

Linguistic competence:
- a or *an*
- Possessives
- Questions and answers with possessives
- Connected discourse (*but*)

1 Learn possessives

A **Listen and read Joe's story. Complete the sentences below.**

> My name is Joe. This is my daughter. Her name is Grace. This is my grandson. He is a great kid. His name is Charlie. Charlie's eyes are brown. His hair is blond. My eyes are green, but brown eyes are my favourite.

1. Charlie's eyes are _____. 2. His hair is _____.

B **Study the chart. Then complete the sentences below. Use the words in parentheses.**

POSSESSIVE ADJECTIVES

Pronouns	Possessive adjectives	Examples
I	my	My eyes are green.
you	your	Your eyes are blue.
he	his	His eyes are brown.
she	her	Her eyes are blue.
it	its	Its eyes are yellow.
we	our	Our eyes are blue.
you	your	Your eyes are brown.
they	their	Their eyes are green.

1. _My_____ eyes are green. (I)   3. _____ eyes are blue. (we)

2. _____ eyes are brown. (he)   4. _____ eyes are green. (they)

C **Look at the pictures in 1A. Circle the correct words.**

1. ((Her) / Their) name is Grace.
2. (His / Her) name is Charlie. His hair (is / are) blond.
3. (Their / Your) names (is / are) Grace and Charlie.
4. Grace is a mother. Charlie is (his / her) son.

☑ Describe people (CLB 2 W, 3 S)

32 ☑ Understand descriptive information about people (CLB 3 L/R)

2 Ask and answer information questions with possessives

A Study the chart. Listen and repeat the questions and answers.

Information questions and answers with possessives		Notes:
A: What colour is Charlie's hair? **B:** His hair is blond.	**A:** What colour is Grace's hair? **B:** Her hair is blond.	Use **'s** after a name for the possessive. Charlie**'s** eyes = his eyes Mary**'s** book = her book Mr. Smith**'s** pen = his pen
A: What colour are Charlie's eyes? **B:** His eyes are brown.	**A:** What colour are Grace's eyes? **B:** Her eyes are blue.	

B Complete the answers.

1. **A:** Who is Charlie's grandfather?

   B: _His_ name is Joe.

2. **A:** Who is Joe's grandson?

   B: Charlie is _____ grandson.

3. **A:** What is his daughter's name?

   B: _____ name is Grace.

4. **A:** What is your teacher's name?

   B: _____ teacher's name is _____.

C Underline the possessive names. Write new sentences.

1. <u>Grace's</u> hair is blond.   _Her hair is blond._ _____

2. Joe's eyes are green.   _____

3. Paulina's children are tall.   _____

4. Grace and Charlie's dog is brown.   _____

3 Practise possessives

A Read the questions. Write your answers in the chart.

Questions	My answers	My partner's answers
1. What's your name?		
2. What colour are your eyes?		
3. What colour is your hair?		

B Interview a partner. Write your partner's answers in the chart.

C Talk about the answers in the chart with your class.

His name is Asim. Asim's eyes are green. His hair is black.

TEST YOURSELF ✔

Close your book. Write 4 sentences. Describe your classmates and your teacher.
My teacher's hair is brown.

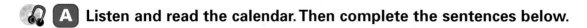

LESSON 4 — Everyday conversation

FOCUS ON

Real-life math:
• Calculate days between events
Socio-cultural competence:
• Social/cultural conventions about birthdays

1 Learn to read and say dates

🎧 **A** Listen and read the calendar. Then complete the sentences below.

March

Sun.	Mon.	Tues.	Wed.	Thurs.	Fri.	Sat.
		1st	🎂 2nd Ashley	3rd	4th	5th
6th	7th	8th	9th	10th	11th	12th
13th	14th	15th	16th	17th	18th	19th
☀ 20th The first day of spring	21st	22nd	🎂 23rd Julie	24th	25th	26th
27th	28th	29th	30th	31st		

Need help?

Months of the year

January	July
February	August
March	September
April	October
May	November
June	December

Dates
1st = first
2nd = second
3rd = third
4th = fourth
5th = fifth
20th = twentieth
21st = twenty-first

1. Ashley's birthday is on _____.
2. The first day of spring is on _____.

🎧 **B** Listen and read.

Ashley: Hello, Ed. It's Ashley. What's the date today?
Ed: It's March 2nd.
Ashley: Well, what day is today? Is it a special day?
Ed: It's Wednesday.
Ashley: Wednesday, March 2nd?
Ed: Yes, that's right. Oh! Happy birthday, Ashley!

🎧 **C** Listen again and repeat.

D Work with a partner. Practise the conversation.
Talk about today.

A: What's the _____ today?
B: It's _____.
A: What _____ is today?
B: It's _____.
A: _____, _____?
B: Yes, that's right.

☑ Ask for and give information about dates (CLB 3 S/L)
34   ☑ Take phone messages (CLB 3 L/W)

2 Practise taking phone messages

 A Listen to the phone messages. Which call is in the evening?

 B Listen again. Then complete the phone messages.

① phone messages

Date:	10/5
Time:	3:00
From:	Tim
Phone number:	555-9241

Please call

② phone messages

Date:	
Time:	
From:	Jackie
Phone number:	

Happy Birthday!

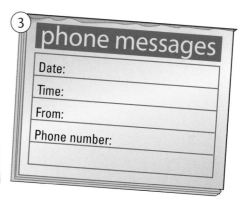

③ phone messages

Date:	
Time:	
From:	
Phone number:	

3 Practise your pronunciation

 A Listen and repeat the numbers in the chart.

-st	-nd	-rd	-th
first	second	third	fourth
twenty-first	twenty-second	twenty-third	twenty-fourth

 B Listen and circle *a* or *b*.

1. a. 1st	2. a. 23rd	3. a. 7th	4. a. 4th	5. a. 1st	6. a. 3rd
b. 3rd	b. 26th	b. 2nd	b. 14th	b. 21st	b. 23rd

C Work with a partner. Look at the calendar on page 34.
Partner A: Say a date. Partner B: Point to the date on the calendar.

4 Real-life math

Complete the sentences about Julie.

The date is March 10th.

Julie's birthday is on March 23rd.

Her birthday is _____ days from today.

Julie

⌐ **TEST YOURSELF** ✔ ¬

Tell a partner the names and birthdays of 3 friends or family members.
Write your partner's information.

1 Get ready to read

A Look at the pictures. Read the words.

1

adult children

2

large family

3

small family

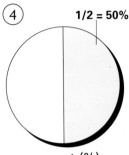
4

1/2 = 50%

percent (%)

B Work with classmates. Answer the questions.

1. What is a large family?
2. What is a small family?

2 Read about Canadian families

A Read the article.

Families

Do you know that in Canada, eleven percent of families are with three or more children? Twenty-seven percent of families are with only one child. Surprise! In thirty-six percent of Canadian families, there are no children at home. These are families with adult children or no children.

- 3+ children
- 2 children
- 1 child
- no children

11%

26%

36%

27%

Source: *Statistics Canada*

B Listen and read the article again.

☑ Interpret information about Canadian families (CLB 3 L/R)
☑ Interpret tables and pie charts (CLB 3/4 R)
36 ☑ Complete simple charts (CLB 2 W)

C Complete the sentences. Use the words in the box.

| at home   twenty-seven   families   ~~children~~ |

1. Eleven percent of families in Canada have three or more ___children___.
2. _____ percent of families in Canada are with one child.
3. Thirty-six percent of families have no children _____.
4. In twenty-six percent of _____, there are two children.

D Match the letters in the chart with the sentences.
Look at the article in 2A for help.

__c__ 1. families with one child
____ 2. families with two children
____ 3. families with three or more children
____ 4. families with no children at home

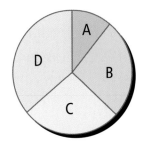

3 Think about family size

A Think about your family. Answer the questions.

1. How many children are there in your home? _____
2. How many adults are there in your home? _____
3. Is your family large or small? _____

B Work with your classmates. Complete the chart.

	Number of children at home			
	1 child	2 children	3 or more children	no children
Number of classmates with:				

C Talk about the answers in the chart with your class.

Five people have one child.

BRING IT TO LIFE

Find pictures of families in newspapers, in magazines, or on the Internet. Bring the pictures to class. Talk about the pictures with your classmates.

1 Grammar

A **Complete the sentences. Use *a* or *an*.**

1. It's __a__ new computer.
2. It's _____ old computer.
3. She's_____ attractive child.
4. He's _____ tall man.
5. It's _____ easy exercise.
6. It's _____ difficult exercise.

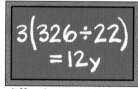

new   old

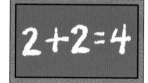

easy   difficult

B **Match the questions with the answers.**

__c__ 1. What colour are Mr. Smith's eyes?   a. Her name is Jan.

____ 2. What colour are his mother's eyes?   b. My class is at 8:00.

____ 3. What is your cousin's name?   c. His eyes are brown.

____ 4. What time is your class?   d. His class is at 10:00.

____ 5. What time is her brother's class?   e. Her hair is brown.

____ 6. What colour is Marta's hair?   f. Her eyes are blue.

C **Work with a partner. Complete the chart. Then say the dates.**

11/2	November 2nd
1/11	January 11th
6/3	
	October 1st

D **Complete the story. Use the words in the box.**

a	are	her	is	our	an	he	his	~~my~~	~~she~~

___My___ name is Jack. Dora is my wife. ___She___ is _____ attractive
   1   2   3

woman. Her eyes _____ green. _____ hair is black. _____ son's
                     4   5   6

name _____ Chris. _____ hair and eyes are brown. _____ is
          7   8   9

_____ good little boy.
  10

2 Group work

A Work with 2–3 classmates. Write 5 sentences about the family on page 29. Talk about the sentences with your class.

His name is Hector. He is Eric's uncle.

B Interview 3 classmates. Write their answers in your notebook.

ASK OR SAY:

1. Name a friend or family member.
2. What colour is his or her hair?
3. What colour are his or her eyes?

> *Classmate–Alan*
> *1. Raisa–sister*
> *2. Her hair is red.*
> *3. Her eyes are green.*

C Talk about the answers with your class.

PROBLEM SOLVING

A Listen and read about Dilip. **What is the problem?**

Today is Dilip's first day of school. This is his new student ID card. Dilip is not happy with the card. There's a problem.

B Work with your classmates. Answer the question. (More than one answer is possible.)

What can Dilip do?

    a. Go to the school office.
    b. Tell the teacher.
    c. Say nothing about it.
    d. Other: _____.

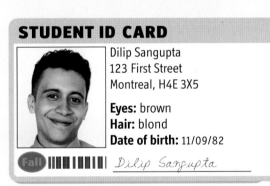

STUDENT ID CARD

Dilip Sangupta
123 First Street
Montreal, H4E 3X5

Eyes: brown
Hair: blond
Date of birth: 11/09/82

Dilip Sangupta

UNIT 4

At Home

FOCUS ON

Critical thinking:
• Describe objects in a room
• Analyse personal activity items
• Decide when to pay bills
• Add utility bills

LESSON 1 **Vocabulary**

1 Learn about places in the home

A Look at the picture. Name the colours.

B Listen and look at the picture.

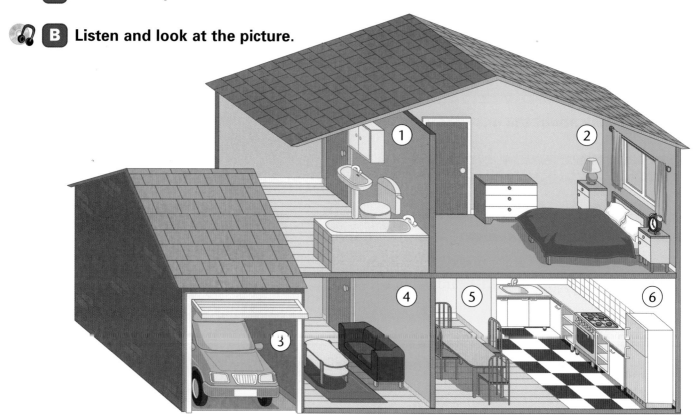

C Listen and repeat the words.

1. bathroom   3. garage   5. dining area
2. bedroom   4. living room 6. kitchen

D Look at the picture. Complete the sentences.

1. The _____kitchen_____ is white.   4. The _____ is grey.
2. The _____ is pink.   5. The _____ is yellow.
3. The _____ is green.   6. The _____ is blue.

☑ Identify rooms in the home, furniture, and appliances (CLB 2 L/R)
☑ Describe location of furniture and appliances (CLB 2 S)
40 ☑ Copy places and things; describe furniture and appliances (CLB 2 W)

2 Talk about things in the home

A Work with your classmates. Match the words with the picture.

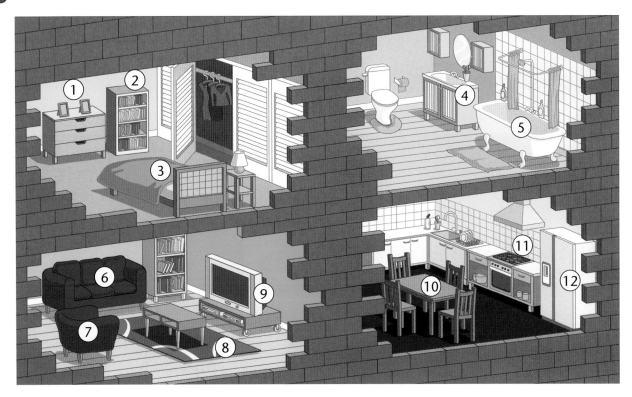

	bathtub		chair		rug		stove
	bed	1	dresser		sink		table
	bookcase		refrigerator		couch		TV (television)

B Listen and check your answers. Then practise the words with a partner.

C Cross out (X) the thing that is NOT usually in these rooms.

1. living room:	couch	TV	sink
2. bedroom:	dresser	stove	b~~e~~d
3. kitchen:	stove	refrigerator	bookcase
4. bathroom:	bed	sink	bathtub

D Work with a partner. Ask and answer questions. Use the picture in 2A.

A: Where is the couch?
B: It's in the living room.

A: Is the stove in the living room?
B: No, it isn't. It's in the kitchen.

TEST YOURSELF ✔

Close your book. Write 4 places and 6 things in the home. Check your spelling in a dictionary.

1 Read about things to do at home

🎧 **A** **Look at the pictures. Listen.**

Sunday at Our Place

🎧 **B** **Listen again. Read the sentences.**

1. My roommates and I go to Adult Learning Centre. We are at home today.
2. Robert is in the yard. He's cutting the grass.
3. Simon is watching TV in the living room.
4. Julio and Luis are in the bedroom. They are playing a video game.
5. And me? I'm cooking dinner and listening to music with my friend.
6. Sundays are great at our place.

C **Check your understanding. Mark the sentences T (true) or F (false).**

___T___ 1. Robert is in the yard.

_____ 2. Simon is cooking in the kitchen.

_____ 3. Julio and Luis are in the bedroom.

_____ 4. Robert is studying.

_____ 5. My friend and I are listening to music in the living room.

☑ Identify places and things to do at home (CLB 3 L/R)

42   ☑ Describe things in the home (CLB 2 S/W)

2 Write about your home

A Look at the pictures on page 42. In your notebook, draw yourself and your family or friends in the rooms of your home.

B Use your picture to write your story.

My _____ and I are at home.

I am in the _____ .

_____ is in the _____ .

It's a _____ day at our home.

> **Need help?**
>
> It's a _____ day.
> good
> great
> special
> nice
> quiet

C Read your story to a partner.

3 Talk about your home

A Listen and look at the pictures.

Singular	
Near	this
Far	that

Plural	
Near	these
Far	those

B Study the charts and the pictures in 3A. Complete the sentences.

1. _This_ is a small TV.
2. _____ is a large TV.
3. _____ are brown chairs.
4. _____ are green chairs.

C Draw your home on the board. Ask and answer questions with your classmates.

A: *What's that?*
B: *This is my kitchen.*

A: *What are those?*
B: *These are my chairs.*

> **TEST YOURSELF** ✔
>
> Close your book. Write 3 sentences about things in your home.
> *My couch is in the living room.*

FOCUS ON

Linguistic competence:
• The present continuous
• Information questions and answers

1 Learn the present continuous

A Look at the pictures. Read the sentences. Who is working?

① Tina is cleaning her home.

② Mark is washing the windows.

③ Jean and Pam are eating lunch.

B Study the charts. Complete the sentences below.

THE PRESENT CONTINUOUS

Statements						
I	am	eating.	We		are	eating.
You	are		You			
He She It	is		They			

Contractions
I am = I'm
I'm eating.
We are = We're
We're eating.

1. I _____ eating.   2. They are _____.

Negative statements						
I	am not	eating.	We		are not	eating.
You	are not		You			
He She It	is not		They			

Contractions
is not = isn't
He isn't eating.
are not = aren't
They aren't eating.

3. He _____ not eating.   4. We are _____ eating.

C Look at the pictures. Complete the sentences.

① ② ③ ④

1. He ___is mopping___ the floor.

2. She _____ the rug.

3. They _____ the furniture.

4. The cat _____ on the rug.

mopping vacuuming dusting sleeping

D Read the sentences to a partner.

☑ Match questions with answers (CLB 2 R)
☑ Describe daily activities (CLB 2 W)

2 Ask and answer information questions

A Study the chart. Listen and repeat the questions and answers.

Information questions and answers	
A: What are you doing? **B:** I'm studying.	**A:** What are you doing? **B:** We're studying.
A: What is he doing? **B:** He's studying.	**A:** What are they doing? **B:** They're studying.

B Match the questions with the answers.

_c_ 1. What are Jean and Pam doing?   a. I'm studying.

____ 2. What is Tina doing?   b. It's sleeping.

____ 3. What is Mark doing?   c. They're eating.

____ 4. What is the cat doing?   d. He's washing the windows.

____ 5. What are you doing?   e. She's cleaning.

C Work with a partner. Complete the sentences with the words in the box.

am writing	~~is reading~~	is playing	are listening	are studying	is sleeping

1. **A:** What is Maria doing?

   B: She _____is reading_____ a book.

2. **A:** What are Janet and Nancy doing?

   B: They _____ to music.

3. **A:** What is Neil doing?

   B: He _____ a video game.

4. **A:** What are you doing?

   B: I _____ sentences.

5. **A:** What is the cat doing?

   B: It _____.

6. **A:** What am I doing?

   B: You _____ English.

3 Practise the present continuous

Work with your classmates. Follow the directions.

Student A: Act out an activity in the box. Don't talk.

Classmates: Guess the activity.

mopping	dusting	cooking	sleeping	vacuuming	studying	eating

TEST YOURSELF ✔

Close your book. Write the answers to the questions: What are you doing?
What is your teacher doing? What are you and your classmates studying?

FOCUS ON

Socio-cultural competence:
• Customs and conventions in shared housing (paying bills)
Functional competence:
• Requesting assistance in writing notes
Real-life math:
• Add utility bill totals

1 Learn about utility bills

A Look at the utility bills.
Complete the sentences below with the due dates.

Acme Electric Company

PAYMENT DUE DATE:

Oct. 1

electric bill

Atlantic Phone Service

PAYMENT DUE DATE:

Oct. 1

phone bill

GLOBE GAS COMPANY

PAYMENT DUE DATE:

Oct. 15

gas bill

West Water Company

PAYMENT DUE DATE:

Oct. 15

water bill

1. Pay the electric bill and phone bill by _____.

2. Pay the gas bill and water bill by _____.

B Listen and write the totals for the utility bills.

1. The gas bill total is $____17.00____.   3. The electric bill total is $_____.

2. The phone bill total is $_____.   4. The water bill total is $_____.

C Listen and read.

A: Can you help me?
B: Sure. What are you doing?
A: I'm writing a note to my roommate. He's not here.
B: OK. Read the note to me.
A: Please pay the gas bill. Tomorrow is the 31st.
B: That sounds good to me.

Please pay the gas bill.

D Listen again and repeat.

E Work with a partner. Practise the conversation. Use your own information.

A: Can you help me?
B: Sure. What are you _____?
A: I'm writing a note to _____. _____ not here.
B: OK. Read the note to me.
A: Please pay the _____. Tomorrow is the _____.
B: That sounds good to me.

☑ Identify details in utility bills (CLB 2 L/R)
☑ Ask for help in writing a note (CLB 3 S)
46 ☑ Write a short note about utility bills (CLB 3 W)

2 Learn subject and object pronouns

A Look at the pictures. Read the sentences.

1. <u>Joe</u> is talking to <u>Mary</u>.
   <u>He</u> is talking to <u>her</u>.

2. <u>Mary</u> is listening to <u>Joe</u>.
   <u>She</u> is listening to <u>him</u>.

3. <u>Mary</u> is paying <u>the bill</u>.
   <u>She</u> is paying <u>it</u>.

Please pay the phone bill today.

B Study the charts.

Subject pronouns	Object pronouns	Subject pronouns	Object pronouns
I	me	we	us
you	you	you	you
he	him	they	them
she	her		
it	it		

C Change the sentences. Use the pronouns in the chart.

1. <u>Martin</u> is writing to <u>Sara</u>. <u>He is writing to her.</u>

2. <u>Jean and Pat</u> are listening to <u>Mark</u>. _____

3. <u>Tina</u> is talking to <u>you and me</u>. _____

4. <u>You and I</u> are listening to <u>our teacher</u>. _____

5. <u>My sister</u> is talking to <u>Simon and Jack</u>. _____

6. I am looking at <u>my book</u>. _____

3 Real-life math

Look at exercise 1B. Add the utility bills. Complete the sentences.

1. The total for the electric bill and the phone bill is $_____.
2. The total for the gas bill and water bill is $_____.
3. The total for all of the utility bills is $_____.

TEST YOURSELF ✔

Write a note to a friend about a utility bill. Read the note to a partner.
Listen to your partner's note.

1 Get ready to read

A Look at the pictures. Read the words. What are the people doing?

 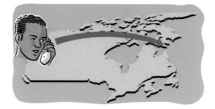 

taking a shower   calling long distance   turning off the lights

B Think about the questions. Check (✔) your answers.

1. How long are your showers?
   ☐ five minutes   ☐ fifteen minutes
   ☐ ten minutes   ☐ twenty minutes

2. How long are your phone calls?
   ☐ five minutes   ☐ twenty minutes
   ☐ ten minutes   ☐ one hour

2 Read about saving money

A Read the website.

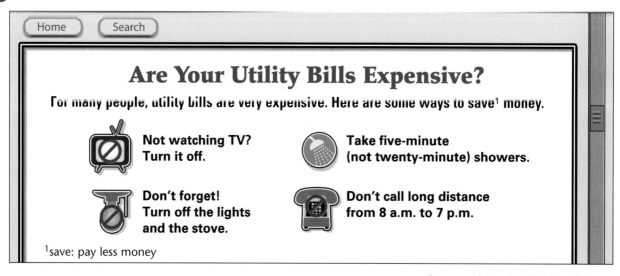

Home   Search

Are Your Utility Bills Expensive?

For many people, utility bills are very expensive. Here are some ways to save[1] money.

🚫📺 **Not watching TV?**
Turn it off.

🚿 **Take five-minute**
(not twenty-minute) showers.

🚫 **Don't forget!**
Turn off the lights
and the stove.

📞 **Don't call long distance**
from 8 a.m. to 7 p.m.

[1]save: pay less money

Source: *Ontario Ministry of Energy*

B Listen and read the website again.

☑ Identify ways to conserve energy (CLB 3 L/R)
☑ Describe bill payments (CLB 3 S)
48 ☑ Address envelopes (CLB 2 W)

C Mark the sentences T (true) or F (false).

_____ 1. Save money. Turn the lights off.

_____ 2. Fluorescent bulbs cost less than regular light bulbs.

_____ 3. Dimmer switches can help you save money.

D Circle the correct words.

1. Some light bulbs use a lot of (energy / money).
2. You can save money on your hydro bill when you use (fluorescent light bulbs / regular light bulbs).
3. To save (dimmer switch / money), turn off your lights.

3 Addressing an envelope

A Look at the envelope. What kind of utility bill is this?

B Look at the envelope. Circle the correct answers.

1. Who is paying the bill?
   a. Atlantic Phone Services
   b. Mavis Clark
   c. Goobies, Newfoundland

2. What is the city in the mailing address?
   a. Goobies
   b. Clark
   c. St. John's

C Think about the questions. Talk about the answers with your class.

1. When do you pay your utility bills?
2. Why is a return address on an envelope important?

BRING IT TO LIFE

Look at a utility bill at home. Address an envelope for the bill or address an envelope for the phone company in 3A. Bring the envelope to class.

Review and expand

1 Grammar

A Circle the correct words.

1. **A:** (Is / **Are**) Ed and Sue eating?
   B: Yes, (we / they) are.
2. **A:** Is Tom (cooking / cook)?
   B: No, he (isn't / aren't).
3. **A:** Is the (rug / girl) sleeping?
   B: No, (it / she) isn't.
4. **A:** (Is / Are) you and Sam studying?
   B: Yes, (I / we) are.

> **Grammar note**
>
> *Yes/No questions and answers*
>
> **A:** Are you working?
> **B:** Yes, I am. *or*
>   No, I'm not.
>
> **A:** Is Mark cooking?
> **B:** Yes, he is. *or*
>   No, he isn't.
>
> **A:** Are you working?
> **B:** Yes, we are. *or*
>   No, we aren't.
>
> **A:** Are they playing?
> **B:** Yes, they are. *or*
>   No, they aren't.

B Write answers for these questions.

1. Are you studying English? _Yes, I am._____
2. Are you mopping the floor? _____
3. Is your teacher eating lunch? _____
4. Are your classmates writing the answers? _____
5. Are you working with a partner? _____

C Write new sentences. Use object pronouns.

1. Janet is talking to <u>Joe</u>.
   _Janet is talking to him._____
2. Jeff is writing to <u>Maria</u>.
   _____
3. Paul is listening to <u>his friends</u>.
   _____
4. Ingrid is talking to <u>Jane and me</u>.
   _____

D Match the questions with the answers.

_b_ 1. Where is she?   a. Yes, he is.
____ 2. What's he doing?   b. She's in the living room.
____ 3. Is he studying English?   c. No, they aren't.
____ 4. What time is it?   d. He's studying.
____ 5. Are Mr. and Mrs. Li at home?   e. It's 6:00.

2 Group work

A Work with 2–3 classmates. Write 5 questions and answers about the picture on page 41. Talk about the sentences with your class.

A: *Where is the sofa?*　　　　A: *Is the sink in the kitchen?*
B: *It's in the living room.*　　B: *Yes, it is.*

B Interview 3 classmates. Write their answers in your notebook.

SAY:

1. Tell me where you study.
2. Tell me where you eat.
3. Tell me where you pay your bills.

> *Classmate—Nancy*
> 1. *in the living room*
> 2. *in the kitchen*
> 3. *in the living room*

C Talk about the answers with your class.

PROBLEM SOLVING

A Listen and read about Mrs. Simms. What is the problem?

The Simms family is at home today. Mrs. Simms is cleaning the house. Her son, Jack, is listening to music. Her daughters, Judy and Joni, are watching TV. Mrs. Simms is tired. She's doing all the work.

B Work with your classmates. Answer the question. (More than one answer is possible.)

What can Mrs. Simms do?
    a. Play video games.
    b. Tell the children to help.
    c. Pay the children to help.
    d. Other: _____

In the Neighbourhood

FOCUS ON
Critical thinking:
• Interpret info from a map
• Label a map
• Ask for and give directions
• Make an emergency exit map
• Determine distance between points on a map

LESSON **1** Vocabulary

1 Learn neighbourhood words

A Look at the map. Say the names of the streets.

B Listen and look at the map.

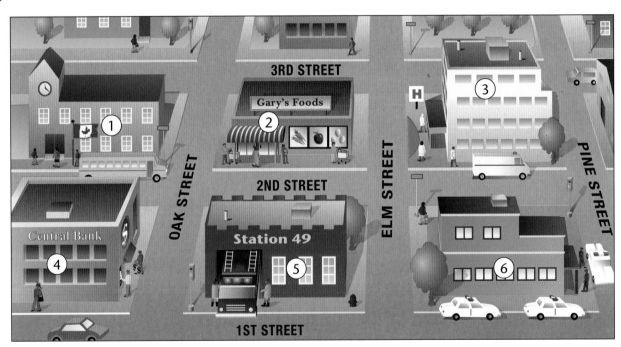

C Listen and repeat the words.

1. school
2. grocery store
3. hospital
4. bank
5. fire station
6. police station

D Look at the map. Complete the sentences.

1. The ___grocery store___ is on 2nd Street.
2. The _____ is on Elm Street.
3. The _____ is on 1st Street.
4. The _____ is on Oak Street.
5. The _____ is on Pine Street.
6. The _____ is on 2nd Street.

☑ Locate neighbourhood places on a map (CLB 3 L/R)
52 ☑ Describe common neighbourhood places (CLB 2, 3 S, 2 W)

2 Talk about transportation and places

A Work with your classmates. Match the words with the picture.

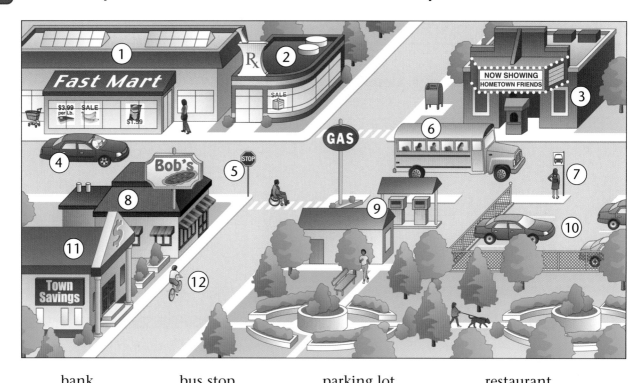

_____ bank   _____ bus stop   _____ parking lot   _____ restaurant

_____ bicycle   _____ car   _____ movie theatre   _____ stop sign

_____ bus   _____ gas station   _____ pharmacy   __1__ supermarket

B Listen and check your answers. Then practise the words with a partner.

C Look at the picture in 2A. Circle the correct words.

1. The boy is riding (a bicycle / a car).
2. The children are riding (a bicycle / the bus).
3. The woman is going to (the pharmacy / the supermarket).
4. The man is driving (a car / a bicycle).
5. The girl is standing at (the bus stop / the stop sign).

D Work with a partner. Practise the conversations. Use the pictures in 1A and 2A.

A: Where is the school?   A: What's the woman doing?

B: It's on 2nd Street.   B: She's going to the supermarket.

TEST YOURSELF ✔

Close your book. Write 5 neighbourhood places and 3 transportation words. Check your spelling in a dictionary.

1 Read about a neighbourhood

A Look at the pictures. Listen.

My Neighbourhood

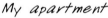

My apartment

My favourite movie theatre

My supermarket

Me

B Listen again. Read the sentences.

1. Let me tell you about my new neighbourhood.
2. My apartment building is on 6th Street. It's next to a little library.
3. There is a big park behind the library.
4. My favourite movie theatre is near my home. It's across from the post office.
5. My supermarket is on Main Street between the bank and the clinic.
6. There is a bus stop in front of my apartment. That's me. I'm waiting for the bus.

next to

behind

in front of

across from

between

C Check your understanding. Mark the sentences T (true) or F (false).

___T___ 1. His apartment is next to the library.

_____ 2. There is a bank behind the library.

_____ 3. The supermarket is on Main Street.

_____ 4. The bus stop is in front of the clinic.

☑ Locate places in the community and on a map (CLB 2, 3 L/R)

54 ☑ Describe own/others' neighbourhood (CLB 2, 3 S/W)

2 Write about your neighbourhood

A Write about your neighbourhood. Complete the sentences.

Let me tell you about my neighbourhood.

My apartment/house is across from _____.

There is a/an _____ next to my home.

There is a/an _____ behind my home.

B Read your sentences to a partner.

3 Talk about locations

A Listen to the directions. Label the map with the words in the box.

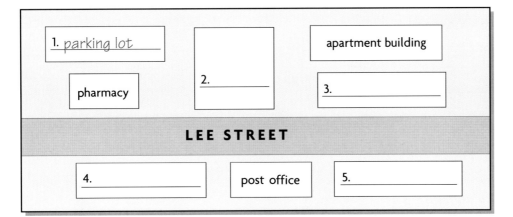

1. parking lot

pharmacy

2.

apartment building

3.

LEE STREET

4.

post office

5.

clinic
fire station
hospital
supermarket
~~parking lot~~

B Look at the map. Circle the correct word.

1. The parking lot is (between / (behind)) the pharmacy.
2. The supermarket is (in front of / on) the apartment building.
3. The pharmacy is (in front of / across from) the hospital.
4. The clinic is (across from / next to) the supermarket.
5. The post office is (between / behind) the hospital and the fire station.

C Listen. Then practise the conversations with a partner. Use your own information.

A: Where is your favourite supermarket?

B: It's on Main Street next to the bank.

A: Where is your favourite restaurant?

B: It's on 1st Street across from the park.

TEST YOURSELF ✔

Close your book. Ask a partner to give the location of 3 places in his or her neighbourhood. Write what you hear.

1 Learn *There is* and *There are*

A **Listen and look at the picture. Read the story. Find Dave in the picture.**

I'm Dave. I live on 4th Street. There are two restaurants on my street. One restaurant is next to my apartment building. There is a nice park across the street. Right now I'm sitting on a bench in the park. It's my favourite place to have lunch.

B **Study the charts. Complete the sentences below.**

THERE IS / THERE ARE

Statements
There is a supermarket on 4th Street.
There are two restaurants.

Negative statements
There isn't a post office.
There aren't any schools.

1. There _____ a supermarket on 4th Street.

2. There _____ two restaurants.

3. There _____ a post office.

4. There _____ any schools.

C **Look at the picture in 1A. Change the sentences from false to true.**

1. There is one restaurant. _There are two restaurants._

2. There's a movie theatre. _____

3. There are two mailboxes. _____

4. There are two gas stations. _____

D **Work with a partner. Use *There is* and *There are* to talk about your classroom.**

There are ten students in the classroom. There's a green notebook on my desk.

☑ Identify details in a neighbourhood (CLB 3 L/R)

56 ☑ Copy sentences using capitalization and punctuation; describe your school's neighbourhood (CLB 2, 3 W)

2 Ask and answer *Yes/No* questions with *there is* and *there are*

A Study the chart. Listen and repeat the questions and answers.

Yes/No questions and answers with *there is* and *there are*	
A: Is there a park on 4th Street? **B:** Yes, there is.	**A:** Are there any restaurants on 4th Street? **B:** Yes, there are.
A: Is there a clinic on 4th Street? **B:** No, there isn't.	**A:** Are there any schools on 4th Street? **B:** No, there aren't.

B Write the questions. Use *Is there* or *Are there*.

1. **A:** _Is there a park on 4th Street?_

   B: Yes, there's a park on 4th Street.

2. **A:** _____

   B: Yes, there is. There's a supermarket on 4th Street.

3. **A:** _____

   B: Yes, there are many people in the park.

4. **A:** _____

   B: No, there isn't. There isn't a pharmacy on 4th Street.

3 Practise *Yes/No* questions with *there is* and *there are*

A Think about your neighbourhood. Complete the questions in the chart. Then write the answers.

Questions	My answers	My partner's answers
1. _Is there_ a library?		
2. _____ a good restaurant?		
3. _____ any bus stops?		

B Interview a partner. Write your partner's answers in the chart.

C Talk about the answers in the chart with your class.

There's a library in my neighbourhood. There isn't a library in Ivan's neighbourhood.

TEST YOURSELF ✔

Close your book. Write 3 sentences about your school's neighbourhood.
Use *there is* and *there are*.

1 Learn directions

A Look at the pictures. Read the directions.

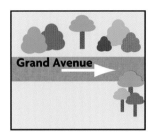

Go straight.

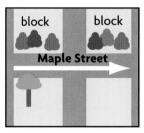

Go two blocks.

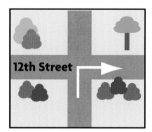

Turn right.

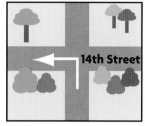

Turn left.

B Listen. Complete the directions to the clinic.

1. Go ___straight___ on Grand Avenue.
2. Turn _____ on 12th Street.
3. Go two _____ on Maple Street.
4. Turn _____ on 14th Street.
5. It's _____ the park.
6. It's _____ to the pharmacy.

C Listen and read.

A: Excuse me. Is there a bank near here?
B: Yes, there is. Go one block on Main Street and turn left on 6th Avenue. The bank is on the corner, next to the clinic.
A: Thanks for your help.
B: No problem. Have a nice day.

D Listen again and repeat each line.

E Work with a partner. Practise the conversation. Use the map.

A: Excuse me. Is there a _____ near here?
B: Yes, there is. Go _____ on _____ and turn _____ on _____. It's on the corner, next to the _____.
A: Thanks for your help.
B: No problem. Have a nice day.

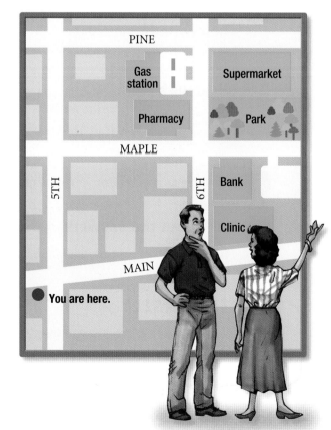

☑ Ask for, give, and follow directions (CLB 3 S/L)
☑ Use a simple map (CLB 3 R)

58

2 Practise your pronunciation

A Listen to the sentences. Listen for the stressed words.

1. The **police** **station** is in **front** of the **park**.
2. It's **across** from the **library**.
3. There's a **restaurant** **next** to the **movie** **theatre**.
4. It's **behind** the **parking** **lot**.

B Listen and underline the stressed words. Read the sentences to a partner.

1. There's a park behind the fire station.
2. The bank is next to the post office.
3. There are two restaurants on the street.
4. The bus stop is in front of the restaurant.

3 Real-life math

A Complete the sentences. How far is it?

1. It's ___400___ km* from Toronto to Ottawa.
2. It's _____ km from Ottawa to Kingston.
3. It's _____ km from Kingston to Hamilton.
4. It's _____ km from Hamilton to London.

*km = kilometre

B Work with a partner.
Make sentences about the map.

It's _____ km from _____
to _____.

Manitoba

Ontario

Quebec

Kenora

Thunder Bay

Sudbury   North Bay

U.S.A.

Ottawa
175 Km
Kingston

400 Km

Toronto
330 km

London   Hamilton
125 km

0   100 mi
0   100 km

TEST YOURSELF ✔

Work with a partner. Partner A: Ask for directions to a place near your school. Partner B: Give the directions. Then change roles.

1 Get ready to read

A Look at the pictures. Read the words.

Home Emergencies

1

Fire

2

Power outage

3

Accident

B Work with your classmates. Make a list of other home emergencies. Ask your teacher for the words you need in English, or use a dictionary.

2 Read about home emergencies

A Read the poster.

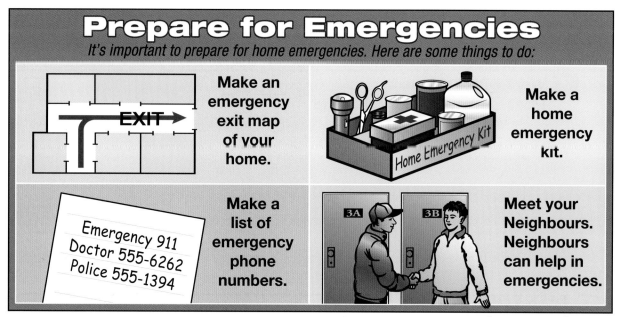

Prepare for Emergencies

It's important to prepare for home emergencies. Here are some things to do:

EXIT →

Make an emergency exit map of your home.

Home Emergency Kit

Make a home emergency kit.

Emergency 911
Doctor 555-6262
Police 555-1394

Make a list of emergency phone numbers.

3A   3B

Meet your Neighbours. Neighbours can help in emergencies.

Source: *www.fema.gov*

B Listen and read the poster again.

☑ Interpret an emergency exit map (CLB 3 R)
60 ☑ Make a home emergency exit map (CLB 3 W)

C Mark the sentences T (true) or F (false).

To prepare for home emergencies:

__T__ 1. Make an exit map for your home.

_____ 2. Make an emergency kit for your teacher.

_____ 3. Call the doctor.

_____ 4. Make a list of emergency phone numbers.

D Complete the sentences. Use the words in the box.

exit	~~prepare~~	neighbours	kit

1. It's important to ___prepare___ for home emergencies.

2. Make an emergency _____ map.

3. Make a home emergency _____.

4. Meet your _____.

3 Read an emergency exit map

A Look at the emergency exit map. Answer the questions below.

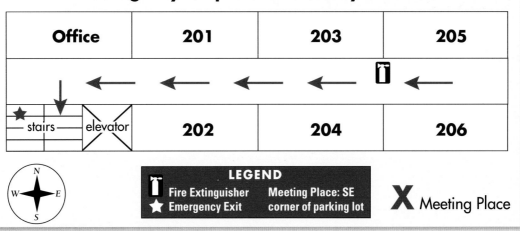

Emergency Map for Blue Valley School

1. Is there an emergency exit in the building? _____

2. Are there any fire extinguishers in the classrooms? _____

B Work with your classmates. Draw an emergency exit map for your classroom.

BRING IT TO LIFE

Work with your family or roommates at home. Make a home emergency exit map. Bring your map to class.

FOCUS ON

Problem solving:
• Determine what to do when lost
Functional competence:
• Convey communicative intent when asking for help
Strategic competence:
• Attitude and approach to overcoming communication breakdown

1 Grammar

A Complete the questions. Then answer the questions. Use your own information.

1. A: How many parks are ____there____ near your school?

   B: There _____ near our school.

2. A: How many good restaurants _____ there near your school?

   B: There _____ near our school.

3. A: How _____ students are there in class today?

   B: _____ in class today.

4. A: _____ many computers are there in your classroom?

   B: There _____ in my classroom.

5. A: How _____ books are there on your desk?

   B: There _____ on my desk.

> **Grammar note**
>
> ***How many?***
> A: How many banks are there on Elm Street?
> B: There is one bank on Elm Street.
>
> A: How many people are there in the park?
> B: There are four people in the park.

B Complete the sentences. Use the words in the box.

to   from   of   in   on

1. The parking lot is next _____to_____ the supermarket.
2. The school is across _____ the hospital.
3. The bus stop is _____ front _____ the apartment building.
4. The park is _____ the corner.

C Unscramble the sentences.

1. a / theatre / on / 1st / movie / There's / Avenue ___There's a movie theatre on 1st Avenue___ .
2. on / the / The / is / park / corner _____ .
3. here / Is / near / there / clinic / a _____ ?
4. the / people / many / in / How / are / park _____ ?
5. street / two / There / gas / my / stations / are / on _____ .

2 Group work

A Work with 2–3 classmates. Write 5 questions about the pictures on page 53. Talk about the questions with your class.

Where is the supermarket?
Is there a bus on the street?

B Interview 3 classmates. Write their answers in your notebook.

ASK:

1. Is there a gas station on your street?
2. Is there a new movie theatre in your neighbourhood?
3. Are there any schools in your neighbourhood?
4. How many supermarkets or grocery stores are there in your neighbourhood?

Classmate—Malaya
1. Yes, there is.
2. No, there isn't.
3. Yes, there are.
4. There are two supermarkets.

C Talk about the answers with your class.

PROBLEM SOLVING

A Listen and read about Jim. What is his problem?

Jim is new in the neighbourhood. His apartment is on Green Street. He is looking for the supermarket, but there's a problem with the directions. Jim is confused.

B Work with your classmates. Answer the question. (More than one answer is possible.)

What can Jim do?
  a. Go to a restaurant and eat.
  b. Ask a neighbour for help.
  c. Go home.
  d. Other: _____

Daily Routines

FOCUS ON

Critical thinking:
- Differentiate between daily and special activities
- Analyse problems and ask for help with an office machine
- Estimate duration of various activities

LESSON 1   Vocabulary

1 Learn everyday activity words

A Look at the pictures. Say the times.

B Listen and look at the pictures.

1 — 7:00 a.m.   **2** — 7:15 a.m.   **3** — 7:30 a.m.

4 — 5:30 p.m.   **5** — 6:00 p.m.   **6** — 11:00 p.m.

C Listen and repeat the words.

1. get up   3. eat breakfast   5. make dinner
2. get dressed   4. come home   6. go to bed

D Look at the pictures. Complete the sentences.

1. They ____go to bed____ at 11:00 p.m.
2. They _____ at 7:15 a.m.
3. They _____ at 6:00 p.m.
4. They _____ at 7:00 a.m.
5. They _____ at 5:30 p.m.
6. They _____ at 7:30 a.m.

☑ Identify and discuss daily routines (CLB 3 S/L)
☑ Write about daily routines (CLB 2 W)

2 Talk about a school day

A Work with your classmates. Match the words with the pictures.

_____ do homework   _____ have lunch   _____ take a shower

_____ do housework   _____ go to bed   _1_ walk to school

_____ drink coffee   _____ ride the bus   _____ work

B Listen and check your answers. Then practise the words with a partner.

C Complete the sentences. Use the words in the box. Use your own information to write the times.

| go | have | ~~take~~ | do | get | come |

1. I _____take_____ a shower at _____.
2. I _____ dressed at _____.
3. I _____ to bed at _____.
4. I _____ home at _____.
5. I _____ lunch at _____.
6. I _____ homework at _____.

D Read your sentences to a partner.

TEST YOURSELF ✔

Close your book. Write the activities you do in the morning, afternoon, and evening. Check your spelling in a dictionary.

1 Read about a work schedule

A Look at the pictures. Listen.

Good morning. Doctor's office.

B Listen again. Read the sentences.

1. My name is Tina Aziz. I work in a doctor's office.
2. This is my work schedule. I work from 9 a.m. to 5 p.m., Monday to Thursday.
3. I turn on the computer and photocopier at 9:00. I answer the phone all day.
4. At noon, I meet my friend. We have lunch and talk.
5. On Fridays, I don't work. I relax. I take my kids to the park.
6. I like my job and my schedule a lot, but Friday is my favourite day.

C Check your understanding. Circle _a_ or _b_.

1. Tina works _____.
   a. four days a week
   b. on Saturday

2. She answers the phone _____.
   a. at 9 a.m.
   b. all day

3. Tina and her friend have lunch _____.
   a. at 11 a.m.
   b. at 12 p.m.

4. She likes her job _____.
   a. a lot
   b. a little

☑ Identify and discuss daily routines and work schedules (CLB 3 S/L/R)

66 ☑ Write a schedule (CLB 2, 3 W)

2 Write about your schedule

A Write about your schedule. Complete the sentences.

I go to school from _____ to _____.

I study _____ at school.

On _____, I relax.

I _____.

Need help?

Ways to relax
go to the park
watch TV
listen to music
talk to friends and family
take a walk

B Read your story to a partner.

3 Talk about a work schedule

A Listen and check (✔) the activities you hear.

_____ 1. mop the floor

_____ 2. vacuum the rug

_____ 3. answer the phone

_____ 4. wash the windows

_____ 5. turn on the photocopier

_____ 6. help the manager

Mel at work

B Listen again. Complete Mel's work schedule.

MORNING 10 A.M.–12 P.M.	AFTERNOON 12 P.M.–3 P.M.
1. _mop the floor_	3. _____
2. _____	4. _____

C Listen and repeat.

A: I work on Saturday and Sunday. How about you?

B: I don't work.

A: I go to school from Monday to Friday. How about you?

B: I go to school on Monday and Wednesday.

D Work with a partner. Practise the conversation. Use your own information.

TEST YOURSELF ✔

Close your book. Listen to your partner's schedule for the week. Write the schedule you hear.

1 Learn the simple present

A Look at the pictures. Read the sentences. What time does she leave for work?

She exercises
at 6:00 a.m.

She has breakfast
at 7:15 a.m.

She brushes her teeth
at 7:30 a.m.

She leaves the house
at 8:00 a.m.

B Study the charts. Complete the sentences below.

THE SIMPLE PRESENT

Statements			
I You	exercise.	We You	exercise.
He She	exercises.	They	

1. He _____. 2. We _____.

Negative statements				Contractions
I You	do not exercise.	We You	do not exercise.	do not = don't I don't exercise.
He She	does not exercise.	They		does not = doesn't He doesn't exercise.

3. You _____ exercise. 4. They do not _____.

C Complete the sentences. Use the words in the box.

~~rides~~   gets   don't   doesn't

1. She ____rides____ the bus every day.

2. He _____ up at 6 a.m.

3. She _____ drink coffee.

4. They _____ have breakfast every morning.

D Read the sentences to a partner.

2 Ask and answer information questions

A Study the chart. Work with a partner. Ask and answer the questions.

Information questions and answers	
A: When do you exercise? **B:** I exercise every day.	**A:** When does he exercise? **B:** He exercises every Saturday.
A: When does she exercise? **B:** She exercises at 6 a.m.	**A:** When do they exercise? **B:** They exercise in the evening.

B Circle the correct word in the questions. Complete the answers.

1. **A:** When (do / does) you get up?

   B: I ___get up___ at 6:30 a.m.

2. **A:** When (do / does) they study?

   B: They _____ every day.

3. **A:** When does (you / she) exercise?

   B: She _____ in the morning.

4. **A:** When (do / does) Joe work?

   B: He _____ every weekend*.

5. **A:** When does Ruby (cook / cooks)?

   B: She _____ every evening.

6. **A:** When (do / does) you study?

   B: I study _____.

*weekend = Saturday and Sunday

3 Practise questions about your day

A Write your answers in the chart.

Questions	My answers	My partner's answers
1. When do you get up?		
2. When do you leave the house?		
3. When do you come home?		
4. When do you make dinner?		

B Interview a partner. Write your partner's answers in the chart.

C Talk about the answers in the chart with your class.

I get up at 6 a.m. Ruby gets up at 7:30.

TEST YOURSELF ✔

Close your book. Write 3 activities you do every day and 3 activities you don't do every day.

FOCUS ON

Socio-cultural competence:
• Conventions of politeness
• Sensitivity to register

1 Learn about office machines and equipment

A Look at the pictures. Read the sentences. Then answer the questions about your classroom.

① Turn on the computer.
Push this button.

② Turn off the printer.
Push this button.

③ Fill the photocopier.
Put the paper here.

④ Fill the stapler.
Put the staples here.

1. Is there a photocopier in your classroom? _No, there isn't._
2. Are there any computers? _____
3. Is there a printer? _____
4. How many staplers are there? _____

B Listen and read.

A: Eva, can you help me?
B: Of course, Paul.
A: How do I turn on the computer?
B: Push this button.
A: Thanks very much, Eva.
B: You're welcome, Paul. That's my job.

C Listen again and repeat.

D Work with a partner. Practise the conversation. Use the information from 1A.

A: _____, can you help me?
B: Yes, _____.
A: How do I _____?
B: _____.
A: Thanks very much.

☑ Identify and respond to requests (CLB 3 L/S)
☑ Give and follow operating instructions (CLB 3 S/L/R)

E Listen and match. Write the number under the picture.

____   ____   1   ____

2 Practise your pronunciation

A Listen to the sentences.

"s"	"z"	"iz"
He helps customers.	He fills the stapler.	He closes the store.
She counts the money.	She cleans offices.	She washes windows.
It prints.	It copies.	It uses staples.

B Read the sentences in the chart.

C Work with a partner. Talk about Miguel's work routine.

He works at the supermarket. He opens the store.

TEST YOURSELF ✔

Work with a partner. Partner A: Ask for help with an office machine.
Partner B: Help your partner. Then change roles.

1 Get ready to read

A Look at the pictures. Read the words.

He sleeps <u>a little</u>.

He sleeps <u>a lot</u>.

B Think about your daily routine. Check (✔) the boxes.

	I work …	I study …	I sleep …	I relax …	I exercise …
a little					
a lot					

C Talk about your daily routine with your classmates. Use the chart.

I work a lot.

2 Read about daily routines in Canada

A Read the article.

WHERE DOES THE TIME GO?

A new study on commuting[1] found that Canadians spend about 12 full days a year getting to work and returning home.

In Toronto, commuters took 79 minutes a day making the round trip between their home and their workplace in 2005. That's about 275 hours of commuting, in a 260-day work year. The people in Montreal took 76 minutes. In fast-growing Calgary, the round trip took 66 minutes.

The study also found that the average travel time rose for both car users and public transit users. But it confirmed what many people already know; it is usually faster to use a car to get to work than public transit.

[1] commuting: travelling to and from work

Source: *Statistics Canada*

B Listen and read the article again.

☑ Identify personal, family, and work responsibilities (CLB 4 L/S/R)

☑ Interpret graphs (CLB 4 R)

C Mark the sentences T (true) or F (false).

_____ 1. Canadians spend a little time commuting.

_____ 2. People in Montreal spend more time commuting than people in Calgary.

_____ 3. In Canada, people go to work about 260 days in a year.

_____ 4. Many people in Canada relax a lot.

D Complete the sentences. Use the words in the box.

commuting travel public transit car

1. Its takes longer to travel by _____ _____ than by car.
2. The study found that Canadians spend about 12 days a year _____.
3. Some Canadians commute by _____.
4. Canadians spend more _____ time getting to work and returning home.

3 Read about paid and unpaid work

A Look at the graph. Complete the sentences.

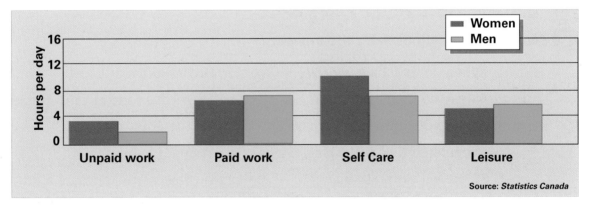

Source: *Statistics Canada*

1. _____ do paid work for seven hours every day.
2. Women enjoy _____ hours of leisure time every day.

B Think about the graph. Talk about the answers with your class.

1. Do men or women spend more time doing unpaid work? Who spends more time doing paid work?
2. How many hours a day do men spend doing self-care? How about women?

⌐ **BRING IT TO LIFE** ⌐

Find pictures of everyday activities. Look in newspapers, magazines, or on the Internet. Bring the pictures to class. Talk about them with your classmates.

FOCUS ON

Problem solving:
• Determine how to solve problems and ask for help in the workplace
Functional competence:
• Convey communicative intent to get the job done

1 Grammar

A Circle *a* or *b*.

1. I _____ lunch at noon.
   a. have
   b. has

2. Marvin _____ breakfast everyday.
   a. have
   b. has

3. Kayla _____ have any free time today.
   a. don't
   b. doesn't

4. Lev and Min _____ have class on Saturday.
   a. don't
   b. doesn't

Grammar note

have

| I You We They | } have free time. don't have free time. |
| He She | } has free time. doesn't have free time. |

B Match the questions with the answers.

_b_ 1. When do they have lunch?

_____ 2. Where do they eat dinner?

_____ 3. When does John have lunch?

_____ 4. When does Kyle make breakfast?

_____ 5. Does Don eat breakfast?

a. He has lunch at noon.

b. They have lunch in the afternoon.

c. Yes, he does.

d. They eat at home.

e. He makes breakfast at 7 a.m.

C Write the questions. Use *When*.

1. **A:** _When does she walk to school?_

   B: She walks to school every afternoon.

2. **A:** _____

   B: I clean the kitchen every Saturday.

3. **A:** _____

   B: They go to the park every weekend.

4. **A:** _____

   B: He rides the bus every day.

5. **A:** _____

   B: We relax every weekend.

2 Group work

A Work with 2–3 classmates. Write 5 questions and answers about the pictures on page 65. Talk about the sentences with your class.

When does she walk to school?
She walks to school in the morning.

B Interview 3 classmates. Write their answers in your notebook.

ASK:

1. When do you get up?
2. When do you have lunch?
3. When do you relax with your family and friends?

> *Classmate—Lara*
> *1. at 6 a.m.*
> *2. in the afternoon*
> *3. every evening*

C Talk about the answers with your class.

PROBLEM SOLVING

A Listen and read about Nick. What is his problem?

Today is Nick's first day at his new job. He works at a bank. He answers the phones and works at a computer. Nick's manager says, "Make 100 copies and staple them for me." Nick doesn't understand the directions on the photocopier.

B Work with your classmates. Answer the question. (More than one answer is possible.)

What can Nick do?
  a. Ask another person to make the copies.
  b. Ask the manager for help.
  c. Open and close all the photocopier doors.
  d. Other: _____

C Work with your classmates. Make a list of things Nick can say.

Shop and Spend

FOCUS ON

Critical thinking:
- Calculate totals of money and personal cheques
- Examine values of coins and bills
- Compare and contrast clothing

LESSON 1 Vocabulary

1 Learn money words

A Look at the pictures. What's the total of the cash?

B Listen and look at the pictures.

Cash

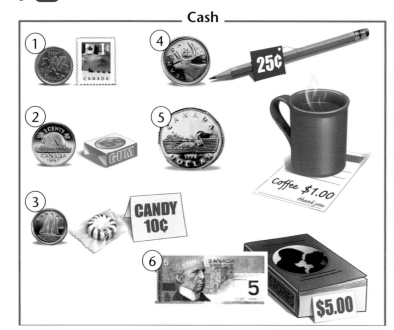

C Listen and repeat the words.

1. penny	3. dime	5. loonie	7. cheque
2. nickel	4. quarter	6. five-dollar bill	8. money order

D Look at the pictures. Complete the sentences.

1. The pencil is 25¢. Pay with a _quarter_.
2. The gum is 5¢. Pay with a _____.
3. The candy is 10¢. Pay with a _____.
4. The stamp is 1¢. Pay with a _____.
5. The rent is $300. Pay with a _____.
6. The book is $5. Pay with a _____.
7. The gas bill is $45. Pay with a _____.
8. The coffee is $1. Pay with a _____.

☑ Identify currency (CLB 1 L/R)
☑ Identify clothing items (CLB 2 L/R)
76 ☑ Copy words related to currency; describe currency (CLB 2 W)

2 Talk about clothes

A Work with your classmates. Match the words with the picture.

____ blouse   <u>1</u> customer   ____ pants   ____ shoes   ____ socks   ____ tie

____ change   ____ dress   ____ shirt   ____ skirt   ____ suit   ____ T-shirt

B Listen and check your answers. Then practise the words with a partner.

C Look at the picture. Match the questions with the answers.

<u>d</u> 1. How much is the dress?   a. $19.99

____ 2. What colour are the shoes?   b. two

____ 3. How much is the shirt?   c. black

____ 4. How many customers are there?   d. $9.99

____ 5. How many people are working?   e. four

D Work with a partner. Ask and answer questions. Use the pictures in 1A and 2A.

A: How much is the pencil?   A: How much are the pants?

B: It's 25¢.   B: They're $24.99.

TEST YOURSELF ✔

Close your book. Write 6 clothing words and 6 money words. Check your spelling in a dictionary.

1 Read about shopping at a mall

A Look at the pictures. Listen.

May I help you?

B Listen again. Read the sentences.

1. It's cold today. I need a new sweater. It's time to go to the mall!
2. I shop at Dan's Discount Store. The salespeople are friendly. The prices are good.
3. I want an inexpensive yellow sweater.
4. I don't like this one. It's yellow, but it's too expensive.
5. This sweater is perfect. It's beautiful, and it's on sale.
6. I usually pay with cash, but I have a new credit card. I'm using it today.

C Check your understanding. Mark the sentences T (true) or F (false).

___T___ 1. She's shopping at the mall.

_____ 2. The salespeople at Dan's are not friendly.

_____ 3. She wants a yellow sweater.

_____ 4. She has a new credit card.

☑ Identify clothing for different occasions (CLB 2 L/R)
☑ Identify methods of purchase (CLB 2 L/R)
78 ☑ Describe what you wear on different occasions (CLB 2 S/W)

2 Write about shopping

A Write about yourself. Complete the sentences.

I (like / don't like) the mall.
I shop at _____.
I need _____.
I want _____.
I usually pay _____.

B Read your story to a partner.

3 Talk about what to wear

A Listen to John talk about his clothes. Write the words you hear.

1. _____
2. _____
3. runners

at home

4. hat
5. uniform
6. belt

at work

7. _____
8. _____
9. _____

on special occasions

B Work with a partner. Look at the pictures. Talk about what John likes to wear.

A: What does John wear at home?

B: He wears a T-shirt and jeans.

C Listen and repeat.

A: What do you wear at home?

B: At home, I wear a T-shirt and jeans.

D Work with a partner. Practise the conversation. Use your own information.

TEST YOURSELF ✔

Close your book. Write 3 sentences about what you wear at home, at work, and on special occasions.

FOCUS ON

Linguistic competence:
• Simple present *yes/no* questions
• *Have, need, want*

1 Learn simple present *Yes/No* questions

A   **Look at the pictures. Read the sentences. Who needs a jacket?**

Jim and Joe have new jackets.

Ann doesn't have a jacket.
She needs a jacket.

Mario has a jacket.
He wants a new jacket.

B   **Study the charts. Complete the sentences below.**

SIMPLE PRESENT *YES/NO* QUESTIONS

Questions			
Do	I you we they	need	a jacket? jackets?
Does	he she		a jacket?

Answers					
Yes,	I you we they	do.	No,	I you we they	don't.
	he she	does.		he she	doesn't.

1. **A:** _____ Ann _____ a jacket?   2. **A:** Do Jim and Joe need _____?

   B: Yes, _____ does.   **B:** No, they _____.

C   **Match the questions with the answers. Use the pictures in 1A.**

_a_ 1. Does Mario have a jacket?   a. Yes, he does.

____ 2. Do Jim and Joe need new jackets?   b. No, he doesn't.

____ 3. Does Mario need a jacket?   c. No, they don't.

____ 4. Does Ann have a jacket?   d. No, she doesn't.

D   **Work with a partner. Ask and answer the questions. Look at the pictures in 1A.**

A: Does Ann want a jacket?

B: Yes, she does.

A: Do Jim and Joe need new jackets?

B: No, they don't.

☑ Describe immediate and future wants and needs (CLB 3 S)
80   ☑ Describe needs (CLB 2 W)

2 Ask and answer simple present *Yes/No* questions

A Complete the answers.

1. A: Does the store have a bathroom?
   B: No, _____ it doesn't _____.

2. A: Do the children have new jeans?
   B: Yes, _____.

3. A: Do Ben and Rosa have a new car?
   B: No, _____.

4. A: Does Sue want a sweater?
   B: Yes, _____.

B Write questions. Use *Do* or *Does.*

1. A: _Do you want new shoes?_
   B: Yes, I do. I want new shoes.

2. A: _____
   B: Yes, they do. They need a computer.

3. A: _____
   B: No, he doesn't need a new suit.

4. A: _____
   B: No, they don't have new shoes.

C Write about what you *have, need,* and *want.* Read your sentences with a partner.

1. I _____ want _____ a new jacket.
2. I _ don't need _ a new car.
3. I _____ a dictionary.
4. I _____ a job.
5. I _____ brown shoes.
6. I _____ a new _____.

3 Practise simple present *Yes/No* questions

A Read the questions. Write your answers in the chart.

Questions	My answers	My partner's answers
1. Do you have new shoes?		
2. Do you need a sweater?		
3. Do you want new clothes?		

B Interview a partner. Write your partner's answers in the chart.

C Talk about the answers in the chart with your class.

Maria has new shoes.

TEST YOURSELF ✔

Write 3 sentences about your partner's answers from 3B.

My partner has new shoes. He doesn't need a sweater. He wants new clothes.

FOCUS ON

Real-life math:
- Calculate amounts of change when paying for items

Functional competence:
- Communicative intent (exchange of information and social interaction between customer and salesperson)

1 Learn to buy clothes

A Look at the clothing ad. Complete the sentences.

1. The ___yellow___ shirt is extra large (XL).
2. The _____ shirt is medium (M).
3. The _____ shirt is large (L).
4. The _____ shirt is small (S).

B Listen and read.

A: Excuse me. How much is this blouse?
B: It's on sale for $16.99. What size do you need?
A: I need a medium.
B: Here's a medium in red.
A: I'll take it.

Here's a medium.

C Listen again and repeat.

D Work with a partner. Practise the conversation. Use the clothing ad in 1A.

A: Excuse me. How much is this _____?
B: It's on sale for _____. What size do you need?
A: I need _____.
B: Here's a/an _____ in _____.
A: I'll take it.

☑ Identify and select clothing based on sizes and prices (CLB 2 L/R)
82 ☑ Ask for, offer, and accept assistance (CLB 3 S/L)

E Look at the pictures. Listen and write the sizes and the prices.

① Size: _____ Price: _____

② Size: _____ Price: _____

Size: _____ Price: _____

③ Size: _____ Price: _____

Size: _____ Price: _____

2 Practise your pronunciation

A Listen for the stress.

-*teen*	thir**teen**	four**teen**	fif**teen**	six**teen**	seven**teen**	eigh**teen**	nine**teen**
-*ty*	**thir**ty	**for**ty	**fif**ty	**six**ty	**seven**ty	**eigh**ty	**nine**ty

B Listen and repeat the numbers.

1. 40   3. 14   5. 90
2. 18   4. 13   6. 60

C Listen and circle the prices you hear. Compare answers with a partner.

1. $15.00   ($50.00)   3. $40.28 $14.28   5. $10.18 $10.80
2. $60.00 $16.00   4. $12.16 $12.60   6. $6.19 $6.90

3 Real-life math

**Look at the receipt and read about Tanya.
Then answer the question.**

Tanya buys a sweater. The total is $19.37.
She gives the salesperson a twenty-dollar bill.
How much is her change? _____

```
****SHOP AND SAVE****
SWEATER            $16.99
TAX                 $2.38

TOTAL              $19.37
```

TEST YOURSELF ✔

Work with a partner. Partner A: You're the customer. Tell your partner what
you want to buy. Partner B: You're the salesperson. Help the customer. Then
change roles.

1 Get ready to read

A Look at the pictures. Read the sentences.

① Put your ATM card in the machine.

② Withdraw your cash.

③ Take your cash, card, and receipt.

④ Count your money.

B Work with your classmates. Put the steps in order.

_____ Withdraw your cash.

_____ Take your cash, card, and receipt.

__1__ Put your ATM card in the machine.

_____ Count your money.

2 Read about ATMs

A Read the article.

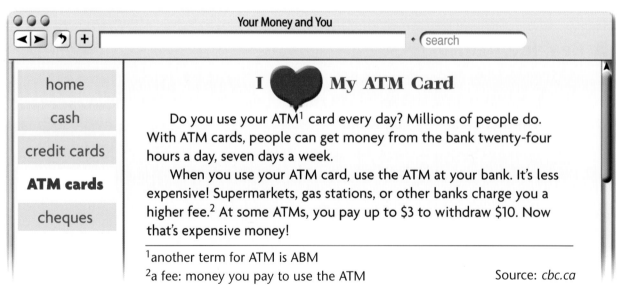

Your Money and You

search

home
cash
credit cards
ATM cards
cheques

I ❤ My ATM Card

Do you use your ATM[1] card every day? Millions of people do. With ATM cards, people can get money from the bank twenty-four hours a day, seven days a week.

When you use your ATM card, use the ATM at your bank. It's less expensive! Supermarkets, gas stations, or other banks charge you a higher fee.[2] At some ATMs, you pay up to $3 to withdraw $10. Now that's expensive money!

[1] another term for ATM is ABM
[2] a fee: money you pay to use the ATM

Source: *cbc.ca*

B Listen and read the article again.

☑ Identify information about using an ATM (CLB 3 L/R)
☑ Interpret a cheque (CLB 2 R)
84 ☑ Describe methods of payment (CLB 3 S)

C Mark the sentences T (true) or F (false).

   T   1. Millions of people use ATM cards every day.

        2. People get money from ATMs seven days a week.

        3. Your bank's ATM charges you a less expensive fee.

        4. All ATMs charge fees.

D Complete the sentences. Use the words in the box.

less expensive	charge	~~ATM card~~	millions

1. Use your _____ATM card_____ to get money from the bank.

2. Your bank's ATM is _____.

3. ATMs at other places often _____ more money.

4. _____ of people use ATM cards.

3 Read a cheque

A Kim Ling is writing a cheque. Look at the cheque. Answer the questions.

KIM LING
218 Green St., Apt. 7
Victoria, BC V9A 1G7

NO. **367**

DATE *April 19, 2008*

PAY TO THE ORDER OF *Shop and Save* $ *31.19*

Thirty-one dollars and nineteen cents   DOLLARS

National Bank   Branch 22
Victoria, BC V8X 2T5

3009421201 053252276

Kim Ling

1. Who is writing the cheque? _____

2. How much money is she paying? _____

3. What store is she paying? _____

B Think about the question. Talk about the answers with your class.

What are some things people pay for with cheques? Name 6 things.

BRING IT TO LIFE

Go shopping. Watch 5 people pay. Do people pay with cash, cheques, or credit cards? Tell your classmates how people pay.

1 Grammar

A **Circle *a* or *b*.**

1. She has ____ new job at the bank.
   (a.) a   b. any

2. Do you have ____ brothers and sisters?
   a. a   b. any

3. We don't have ____ credit cards.
   a. a   b. any

4. I have ____ good friends.
   a. a   b. some

5. Does he have ____ new shirt?
   a. a   b. some

> **Grammar note**
>
> ***a*, *some*, and *any***
>
> **Singular: *a***
>
> A: Do you have a jacket?
> B: Yes, I have a jacket. *or*
>   No, I don't have a jacket.
>
> **Plural: *any/some***
>
> A: Do you have any socks?
> B: Yes, I have some socks. *or*
>   No, I don't have any socks.

B **Match the questions with the answers.**

_c_ 1. Do you want a new jacket?   a. No, she doesn't.

____ 2. Is there an ATM near here?   b. Yes, there are.

____ 3. Do they need new books?   c. Yes, I do.

____ 4. Does she have a new car?   d. No, they don't.

____ 5. Does he like to shop?   e. Yes, he does.

____ 6. Are there any shirts on sale?   f. No, there isn't.

C **Write the answers.**

1. What do they want for dinner? (pizza) _They want pizza._

2. How much money does Pedro have? ($100) _____

3. What colour suit does he want? (blue) _____

4. What do they need? (a new car) _____

5. When do you have lunch? (at 12:30 p.m.) _____

D **Complete the story. Circle the correct words.**

Today Emily ((is) / has) at the mall. She needs (some / any) new shoes. She
                  1   2
(want / wants) inexpensive brown shoes. There are some nice brown shoes (in / on) sale
       3   4
for $25. Emily (has / want) $40. She pays the (customer / salesperson). Her change
                      5   6
(is / are) $15. She (have / likes) her new shoes.
    7   8

2 Group work

A Work with 2–3 classmates. Write 5 sentences about the picture on page 77. Talk about the sentences with your class.

A man is wearing a suit. A woman is buying a dress.

B Interview 3 classmates. Write their answers in your notebook.

ASK:

1. Do you have a favourite clothing store?
2. Do you want any new clothes?
3. Do you need any new work or school clothes?
4. Do you pay for clothes with cash, cheques, or credit cards?

Classmate—Leticia
1. Yes, she does.
2. Yes, she does.
3. No, she doesn't.
4. cash

C Talk about the answers with your class.

PROBLEM SOLVING

A Listen and read about Joel. What is his problem?

Joel is at the bank. He wants $40. He puts his card in the ATM. He takes his card, his money, and his receipt. When he counts the money, he only has $20!

B Work with your classmates. Answer the question. (More than one answer may be possible.)

What can Joel do?
    a. Call the police.
    b. Put the card in the machine again.
    c. Ask for help at the bank.
    d. Other: _____

C Work with your classmates. Make a list of things Joel can say.

Eating Well

LESSON **1** Vocabulary

1 Learn grocery shopping words

A Look at the picture. Where are the people?

B Listen and look at the picture.

C Listen and repeat the words.

1. fruit   2. vegetables   3. basket   4. cart   5. cashier   6. bagger

D Look at the picture. Complete the sentences.

1. The man in the white shirt is next to the __vegetables__ , on the right.

2. The _____ is next to the vegetables, on the left.

3. The _____ has a yellow tie.

4. One woman has a red _____.

5. One man has a blue _____.

6. The _____ has a green blouse.

☑ Identify food items in a grocery store (CLB 2 L/R)
☑ Give a basic description of everyday food items (CLB 2 S)
88 ☑ Describe food shopping (CLB 1 W)

2 Talk about a supermarket

A Work with your classmates. Match the words with the picture.

____ apples   ____ chicken   ____ lettuce   ____ potatoes

_1_ bananas   ____ eggs   ____ milk   ____ soup

____ bread   ____ grapes   ____ onions   ____ tomatoes

B Listen and check your answers. Then practise the words with a partner.

C Cross out (X) the item that does NOT belong in each group.

1. apples   bananas   ~~lettuce~~   grapes
2. cashier   eggs   bagger   customer
3. bread   onions   potatoes   lettuce
4. chicken   bread   soup   cart

D Work with a partner. Talk about grocery shopping.

I buy milk, eggs, bread, and fruit every week.

I use a basket. I pay with a credit card.

How about you?

TEST YOURSELF ✔

Close your book. Write 5 food words and 5 supermarket words. Check your spelling in a dictionary.

1 Read about grocery shopping

A Look at the pictures. Listen.

B Listen again. Read the sentences.

1. The Garcias make a shopping list every Wednesday night.
2. They go to the grocery store every Thursday morning.
3. Mr. Garcia loves oranges. They get oranges every time they shop.
4. Every week, they buy chicken and fish.
5. Once or twice a month, they buy cookies or ice cream.
6. They always look for good prices.

C Check your understanding. Mark the sentences T (true) or F (false).

___T___ 1. The Garcias go to the grocery store every Thursday.

_____ 2. They make a shopping list every Monday.

_____ 3. They buy chicken every week.

_____ 4. Mr. Garcia doesn't like oranges.

_____ 5. They buy cookies every day.

_____ 6. They look for groceries on sale.

☑ Identify shopping habits (CLB 2 L/R)
☑ Interpret food advertisements (CLB 3 L/R)
90 ☑ Make a shopping list (CLB 2 W)

2 Write about grocery shopping

A Write about yourself. Complete the sentences.

I go to the supermarket every _____ .

Every week, I buy _____ , _____ ,

and _____ .

I love _____ .

I always look for _____ .

Need help?

I buy…
eggs.
bread.
milk.

B Read your story to a partner.

3 Talk about grocery shopping

A Look at the supermarket ads. Read the items and the prices.

B Listen to the Garcias talk about the supermarket ads.
Check (✔) the items they are going to buy.

C Listen. Then practise the conversation with a partner.

A: Let's make vegetable soup.

B: We need some onions. Do we need any potatoes?

A: Yes, we do. Do we need any carrots?

B: No, we have some.

salad   fruit salad   spaghetti

TEST YOURSELF ✔

Close your book. Write a shopping list. Tell a partner what's on your list.

1 Learn frequency expressions

A **Look at Lucy's schedule. Answer the questions below.**

Sunday	Monday	Tuesday	Wednesday	Thursday	Friday	Saturday
cook dinner at home	have dinner with Alex	cook dinner at home	cook dinner at home	order pizza		have dinner with Alex

1. Does Lucy have dinner with Alex on Tuesdays and Saturdays? _____

2. When does Lucy order pizza? _____

B **Study the charts.**

FREQUENCY EXPRESSIONS

Frequency expressions	
I cook	every day.
Mary goes shopping	once a week.
We buy cookies	twice a month.
They order pizza	three times a year.

More frequency expressions
every day / week / month / year
once a day / week / month / year
twice a day / week / month / year
three times a day / week / month / year
never (0 times) *We never cook.*

C **Complete the sentences. Use Lucy's schedule in 1A.**

1. Lucy orders pizza _once a week_.
2. Lucy has dinner with Alex _____.
3. Lucy cooks dinner _____.
4. Lucy _____ cooks dinner on Friday.

D **Write sentences with your own information. Read the sentences to a partner.**

1. (cook dinner) _I cook dinner three times a week._
2. (eat dinner at home) _____
3. (eat lunch with friends) _____
4. (have breakfast at home) _____

2 Ask and answer questions with *How often*

A Study the chart. Ask and answer the questions.

Questions and answers with *How often*	
A: How often do you cook? **B:** I cook three times a day.	**A:** How often does he cook? **B:** He cooks twice a week.
A: How often do you cook? **B:** We cook every evening.	**A:** How often does she cook? **B:** She never cooks.

B Complete the questions. Then match the questions with the answers. Use the schedule from 1A.

_____ 1. How _____ does Lucy order pizza?   a. twice a week

_____ 2. How often do Lucy and Alex _____ dinner?   b. never

_____ 3. How often _____ Lucy cook on Fridays?   c. once a week

3 Practise questions about routines

A Read the questions. Write your answers in the chart.

Questions	My answers	My partner's answers
1. How often do you eat dinner with friends?		
2. How often do you order pizza?		
3. How often do you eat dinner at a restaurant?		
4. How often do you cook dinner at home?		

B Interview a partner. Write your partner's answers in the chart.

C Talk about the answers in the chart with your class.

I eat dinner with friends once a week. Mia eats dinner with friends three times a week.

TEST YOURSELF ✔

Write 4 sentences about your partner's answers from 3B.

Martin cooks dinner at home three times a week. He orders pizza once a week.

1 Learn to order food

A **Look at the menu. Write the prices.**

Pappa's Pizza Place

Menu

Pizza

Small pizza $6.50   Medium pizza $8.50   Large pizza $12.00

Drinks

Pop   Iced Tea
Small $1.50 Medium $1.75 Large $2.00

Toppings $1.00 each
pepperoni   onions
mushrooms   peppers

1. A large pepperoni pizza is ___$13.00___ .

2. A medium mushroom pizza is _____ .

3. A small pizza with peppers and onions is _____ .

4. A medium pepperoni and mushroom pizza is _____ .

B **Listen and read.**

A: Are you ready to order?

B: Yes, I am—a medium pizza with onions, please.

A: Do you want anything to drink?

B: Yes, I do. I'd like a small iced tea.

A: OK, that's one medium pizza with onions and
   a small iced tea.

B: That's right.

C **Listen again and repeat.**

D **Work with a partner. Practise the conversation. Use the menu in 1A.**

A: Are you ready to order?

B: Yes, I am—a _____ pizza with _____, please.

A: Do you want anything to drink?

B: Yes, I do. I'd like _____ .

A: OK, that's one _____ pizza with _____
   and _____ .

B: That's right.

☑ Identify and respond to requests when ordering meals (CLB 2 L)
☑ Understand basic menus (CLB 2 L/R)
☑ Order meals from basic menus (CLB 2, 3 S)

🎧 **E** **Listen and complete the orders.**

① **GUEST CHECK**

Date	Table	Guests	Server	128354

_____ large pizzas
with onions
1 _____ pizza with
pepperoni
_____ _____ pop

Total

Thank you! Please come again.

② **Guest Check**

Date	Table	Guests	Server	7742

_____ _____
pizza with peppers
_____ _____
iced teas
_____ _____
_____

Total

Thank you! Please come again.

③ **GUEST CHECK**

Date	Table	Guests	Server	410121

_____ _____
pizzas with _____
and _____
_____ small _____
_____ _____
_____

Total

Thank you! Please come again.

2 Practise your pronunciation

🎧 **A** **Listen to the question and answer.**

A: Are you ready to order? ↗

B: Yes, I am. ↘

🎧 **B** **Listen and circle _question_ or _answer_.**

1. question (answer)   3. question   answer
2. question   answer   4. question   answer

C **Match the questions with the answers. Then practise with a partner.**

_____ 1. Are you ready to order?   a. I want a small pop.
_____ 2. Do you want any toppings?   b. Yes, I am.
_____ 3. Do you want anything to drink?   c. Yes, I do. Mushrooms, please.

3 Real-life math

Write the prices and the totals for the orders in 1E.
Use the menu in 1A.

TEST YOURSELF ✔

Work with a partner. Look at the menu on page 94. Partner A: Order a pizza
and a drink. Partner B: Repeat the order. Then change roles.

1 Get ready to read

A **Read the definitions.**

healthy: something that is good for your body

unhealthy: something that is not good for your body

B **Work with your classmates. Complete the chart with healthy food.**

Healthy food	
apples	

C **Circle the food in the chart that you eat every week.**

2 Read about healthy food

A **Read the article.**

Eating Well with Fruit and Vegetables

Vegetables and fruit have vitamins and minerals.[1] They are usually low in fat and calories.

Canada's Food Guide helps people choose healthy food. It has four food groups – vegetables and fruit, grain, milk, and meat. It recommends that Canadians:

_____
[1] minerals: something that the body needs to be healthy

- Eat one dark green and one orange vegetable each day
- Eat vegetables and fruit with no fat, sugar, or salt
- Eat vegetables and fruit more often than drinking vegetable or fruit juice

Don't eat a lot of unhealthy food. Eat fruit and vegetables every day and be healthy!

Source: *Canada's Food Guide*

B **Listen and read the article again.**

☑ Make a list of healthy food items (CLB 2 W)

☑ Identify healthy eating habits (CLB 3 S/L/R)

☑ Interpret nutrition labels (CLB 3 R)

C Mark the sentences T (true) or F (false).

_T_ 1. Fruit and vegetables have vitamins and minerals.

____ 2. Fruit and vegetables are unhealthy.

____ 3. Eating dark green and orange vegetables is unhealthy.

____ 4. Eat vegetables with no fat, salt, or sugar.

D Complete the sentences. Use the words in the box.

| fruit | ~~healthy~~ | dark green | minerals | vegetables |

1. Eat ___healthy___ food.

2. Vegetables and fruit have vitamins and _____.

3. _____ and _____ are good for you.

4. Eat _____ _____ and orange vegetables.

3 Read food labels

A Work with your classmates. Write the names of the soups.

① Ingredients
water,
tomatoes,
salt

_____tomato soup_____

② Ingredients
water,
chicken,
onions,
carrots

Salt Free!

_____

③ Ingredients
water,
onions,
carrots,
mushrooms,
peppers,
tomatoes,
salt

_____

B Look at the food labels. Complete the sentences.

1. The ___chicken___ soup has no salt.

2. The _____ soup has a lot of vegetables.

3. The _____ soup has three ingredients.

C Think about the questions. Talk about the answers with your class.

1. Do you think it's important to read food labels? Why or why not?

2. How often do you read the labels on food you buy?

BRING IT TO LIFE

Bring a food label to class. Talk about the ingredients with your classmates.
Find out how much food you need every day from Canada's Food Guide on
the Internet. Discuss it with your classmates.

1 Grammar

A **Circle the correct words.**

1. I study ((every) / twice) day.
2. She (always / once) buys apples.
3. They (usually / three times) ride the bus.
4. Pat washes the windows (twice / one) a year.
5. They shop (always / once) a week.
6. Sharon pays the bills (never / three times) a month.

Grammar note

Adverbs of frequency

always ▲ 100%
usually
sometimes
never ▼ 0%

I always eat breakfast.
I usually eat eggs for breakfast.
I sometimes eat breakfast at home.
I never eat pizza for breakfast.

B **Match the sentences with the frequency expressions.**

__e__ 1. Frank watches a movie every Friday.

____ 2. Beth cleans the garage in May and October.

____ 3. She goes to the bank on the 1st and 15th of the month.

____ 4. I feed the cat in the morning, at noon, and at night.

____ 5. Gary and Elaine don't drink pop.

____ 6. She brushes her teeth in the morning and at night.

a. twice a day

b. twice a month

c. twice a year

d. three times a day

e. once a week

f. never

C **Unscramble the sentences.**

1. never / Lucy / Sunday / eats / on / dinner _Lucy never eats dinner on Sunday._
2. eats / once / Mrs. Mack / a week / ice cream _____
3. twice / Ben / does / homework / a week / usually _____
4. Sherman / a week / three / exercises / times _____
5. always / Alicia / English / speaks / at home _____

D **Write the answers.**

1. How often do you go shopping? _I go shopping twice a week._
2. How often do you buy ice cream? _____
3. How often do you cook dinner for friends? _____
4. How often do you clean the kitchen? _____

2 Group work

A **Work with 2–3 classmates. Look at the picture on page 89. Write 5 *How often?* questions about the food in the picture. Talk about the questions with your class.**

How often do you buy bread? How often do you buy oranges?

B **Interview 3 classmates. Write their answers in your notebook.**

ASK:
1. How often do you eat vegetables with your dinner?
2. How often do you order pizza?
3. How often do you cook dinner?

> *Classmate–Ching Fu*
> *1. every day*
> *2. once or twice a month*
> *3. never*

C **Talk about the answers with your class.**

PROBLEM SOLVING

A **Listen and read about the Ruzika family. What is the problem?**

Sam and Lia Ruzika have two daughters. Every night at dinner the children say, "We don't like vegetables." Lia and Sam think, "Our girls need vegetables." Lia cooks different vegetables every night. She cooks broccoli, mushrooms, potatoes, and carrots. The girls never eat them. They say the same thing, "We don't like vegetables."

B **Work with your classmates. Answer the question. (More than one answer is possible.)**

What can Lia and Sam do?
   a. Order pizza with vegetables on it.
   b. Tell the girls that vegetables are healthy.
   c. Give the girls a lot of fruit.
   d. Other: _____

C **Work with your classmates. Make a list of things Lia and Sam can say.**

Your Health

FOCUS ON

Critical thinking:
- Analyse and compare medical advice
- Classify obligations by level of importance
- Interpret a schedule to make appointments
- Interpret warnings on medicine labels

LESSON 1 Vocabulary

1 Learn about parts of the body

A Look at the pictures. Is Mr. Patel healthy?

B Listen and look at the pictures.

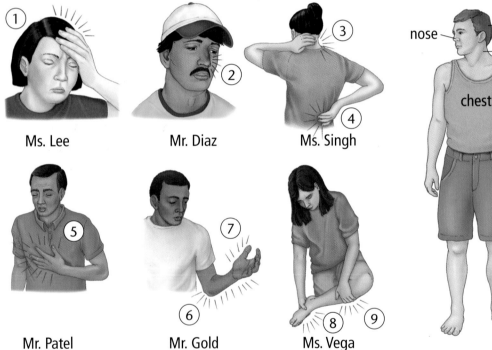

Ms. Lee   Mr. Diaz   Ms. Singh

Mr. Patel   Mr. Gold   Ms. Vega

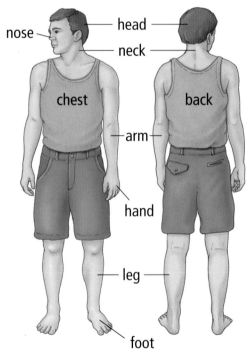

nose — head — neck — chest — back — arm — hand — leg — foot

C Listen and repeat the words.

1. head	3. neck	5. chest	7. hand	9. leg
2. nose	4. back	6. arm	8. foot*	

*one foot / two feet

D Look at the pictures. Complete the sentences.

1. Ms. Lee's ___head___ hurts.   4. Ms. Singh's _____ and _____ hurt.

2. Mr. Diaz's _____ hurts.   5. Mr. Gold's _____ and _____ hurt.

3. Mr. Patel's _____ hurts.   6. Ms. Vega's _____ and _____ hurt.

☑ Identify parts of the body, illnesses, and injuries (CLB 2 L/R)

100 ☑ Describe body parts, illnesses, and injury words (CLB 2 S/W)

2 Talk about a doctor's office

A Work with your classmates. Match the words with the picture.

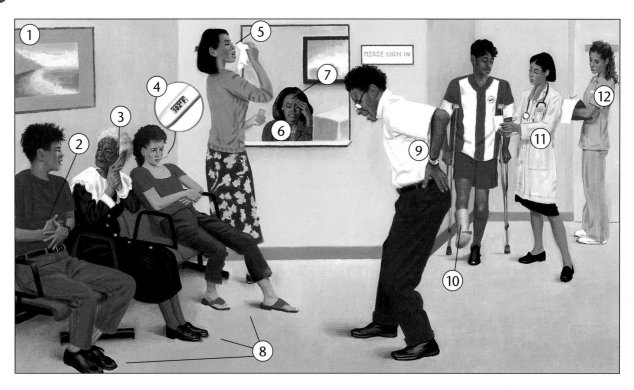

____ backache	____ doctor	____ fever	____ patients
____ broken leg	_1_ doctor's office	____ headache	____ receptionist
____ cold	____ earache	____ nurse	____ stomach ache

B Listen and check your answers. Then practise the words with a partner.

C Cross out (X) the item that does NOT belong in each group.

1. nurse   ~~stomach ache~~   receptionist   doctor
2. patients   earache   stomach ache   headache
3. eyes   mouth   cold   nose
4. arms   legs   nose   hands

D Work with a partner. Ask and answer questions. Use the picture in 2A.

A: What's the matter with the man in the white shirt?

B: He has a backache. What's the matter with the receptionist?

A: Her head hurts. She has a headache.

TEST YOURSELF ✔

Close your book. Write 6 body words and 4 illness and injury words. Check your spelling in a dictionary.

1 Read about a doctor's appointment

A Look at the pictures. Listen.

  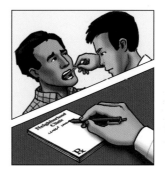 

B Listen again. Read the sentences.

1. Miguel is sick today. He's at the doctor's office. He has a sore throat.
2. He gives his health card to the receptionist.
3. The nurse takes his temperature and his blood pressure.
4. Miguel opens his mouth. The doctor examines him and writes a prescription.
5. Miguel has to take his prescription medicine twice a day.
6. Miguel has to stay home and rest. He wants to get well.

C Check your understanding. Circle the correct words.

1. Miguel has a sore (throat / mouth).
2. Miguel needs his health (car / card).
3. The nurse takes his (temperature / medicine).
4. The doctor examines (him / a prescription).
5. Miguel has to take prescription medicine (once / twice) a day.
6. Miguel has to stay home and (rest / chest).

2 Write about yourself

A Write your story. Complete the sentences.

Sometimes I have a /an _____, and I go to the
doctor. _____ takes my temperature and blood
pressure. _____ examines me and gives me a
prescription. I _____ to get well.

Need help?

Ways to get well
stay home
rest
take medicine

B Read your story to a partner.

☑ Identify procedures in a medical exam; identify medical advice (CLB 2 L/R)
☑ Talk about medical advice (CLB 3 S)
102 ☑ Describe a medical exam (CLB 3 W)

3 Talk about ways to get well and to stay healthy

A Look at the pictures. Read the ways to get well and to stay healthy.

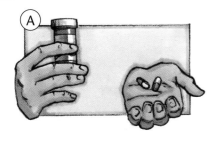

Take medicine.

Rest.

Change your diet.

Exercise.

Drink fluids.

Quit smoking.

B Listen to the conversations. Match the doctor's advice in 3A with the correct patients.

1. Mr. Jones __c__
2. Mrs. Lynn _____
3. Mr. Martinez _____
4. Ms. Mendoza _____
5. Mr. White _____
6. Mr. Wang _____

C Listen and repeat.

A: What do you do for a sore throat?
B: I take medicine. What do you do?
A: I drink tea.

D Work with a partner. Practise the conversation. Use your own ideas.

TEST YOURSELF ✔

Close your book. Tell a partner 3 ways to get well. Change roles. Listen and write your partner's ideas.

1 Learn *have to*

A Look at the pictures. Read the sentences. Where does Jeff have to go?

① Maria has to leave class early.
She has to pick up her son.

② I have a toothache.

Jeff has to leave work early.
He has to go to the dentist.

③ We have a test tomorrow.

Kim and Rosa have to leave the party early. They have to study.

B Study the chart. Complete the sentences below.

HAVE TO

Statements					
I You	have to	go to the dentist.	We You	have to	go to the dentist.
He She	has to		They		

1. He _____ go to the dentist. 2. They _____ go to the dentist.

C Look at the pictures. Circle the correct words.

1. Maria (has / has to) a son.
2. Jeff (has to / have to) go to the dentist.
3. He (has to / has) a toothache.
4. Kim and Rosa (has to / have to) study.
5. They (have / have to) a test tomorrow.
6. They (have / have to) leave early.

D Work with a partner. Talk about things you have to do this week.

A: *I have to study. How about you?*

B: *I have to go to the bank.*

✔ Describe obligations (CLB 3 S)

104   ✔ Write about things you have to do (CLB 2 W)

2 Ask and answer information questions with *have to*

A Study the chart. Ask and answer the questions.

Information questions and answers with *have to*	
A: Why do you have to leave early? **B:** I have to pick up my children.	**A:** Why does he have to leave early? **B:** He has to go to the doctor.
A: Why do they have to leave early? **B:** They have to study.	**A:** Why does she have to leave early? **B:** She has to go to the dentist.

B Match the questions with the answers.

___d___ 1. Why do you have to leave early?   a. She has to leave early.

_____ 2. Why does Jeff have to go to the dentist?   b. He has a sore throat.

_____ 3. Why does Maria have to talk to the teacher?   c. They have to study.

_____ 4. Why do the girls have to go to the library?   d. I have to pick up my son.

_____ 5. Why does Miguel have to see the doctor?   e. He has a toothache.

3 Practise *have to*

A Complete the questions with the words in the box.
Then write your answers.

~~Why~~	What	When	Where

1. __Why___ do you have to come to class every day? _I have to practise English._

2. _____ do you have to do after class today? _____

3. _____ do you have to go after class? _____

4. _____ do you have to get up tomorrow? _____

B Ask and answer the questions in 3A with a partner. Then write 4
sentences about your partner's answers.

Teresa has to practise English.

C Talk about the sentences with your class.

Teresa has to practise English. She has to make lunch after class.

TEST YOURSELF ✔

Close your book. Write 5 things you have to do this week. Use complete
sentences.

FOCUS ON

Socio-cultural competence:
• Customs in making and
  negotiating medical appointments

1 Learn to make an appointment

A **Read the appointment card. Answer the questions.**

> Dear _Vera_ ,
>
> ## YOU HAVE AN APPOINTMENT
>
> With: _Dr. Brown_
>
> On: _Monday, May 12th_
>
> At: _3:00_ a.m. (p.m)
>
> See you then!
>
> (M) T W TH F

1. Who has an appointment with Dr. Brown? _____Vera_____

2. What day is the appointment? _____

3. What's the date of the appointment? _____

4. What time is the appointment? _____

B **Listen and read.**

A: Hello, doctor's office.

B: Hello. This is Carl Lee. I have a terrible cold.
   I have to see the doctor.

A: Let's see. I have an opening on Wednesday at 2:00.
   Is that OK?

B: Yes, it is. Thanks.

A: OK. See you on Wednesday, May 12th at 2:00.

C **Listen again and repeat.**

D **Work with a partner. Practise the conversation. Use your own
information.**

A: I have a terrible _____. I have to see the doctor.

B: Let's see. I have an opening on _____
   at _____. Is that OK?

A: Yes, it is. Thanks.

B: OK. See you on _____ at _____.

☑ Make medical appointments (CLB 3 S/L)

E Listen and complete the appointment cards.

① Dear _Tom_ ,

YOU HAVE AN APPOINTMENT

With: _Dr. Wu_

On: _____

At: _____ a.m. p.m

M   T   W   TH   F

② Dear _____ ,

YOU HAVE AN APPOINTMENT

With: _____

On: _____

At: _____ a.m. p.m

M   T   W   TH   F

2 Learn prepositions *on* and *at*

A Complete the sentences with *on* or *at*.

1. I have to leave _____*at*_____ 5:00.

2. Sue has an appointment _____ Tuesday.

3. We want to go to the party _____ 7:00.

4. I have to see the doctor _____ June 17th.

> **Grammar note**
>
> ***on* or *at*?**
>
> Use *on* for days and dates.
>   on Monday
>   on November 11th
>
> Use *at* for times.
>   at 10:30
>   at noon

B Write your answers.

1. When do you have to come to class? _____

2. When do you have to go to work? _____

3. When do you have to get up tomorrow? _____

3 Practise your pronunciation

A Listen to the sentences.

1. I **have to** see the doctor.
   I **have a** cold.

2. She **has to** go at 2:30.
   She **has a** new job.

B Listen again and repeat.

C Listen and circle the words you hear.

1. (have to)   have   3. has to   has

2. have to   has to   4. have   has

┌─ **TEST YOURSELF** ✔ ─────────────────────

Work with a partner. Make an appointment to see a doctor. Partner A:
You're the patient. Partner B: You're the receptionist. Then change roles.

1 Get ready to read

A **Look at the picture. Read the definitions.**

checkup: a medical examination to check your health when you are not sick

over-the-counter medicine: medicine you don't need a prescription to buy

B **Work with your classmates. How often do you do these things?**

1. exercise   2. eat healthy food   3. get a checkup

2 Read about good health

A **Read the article.**

Feeling Fine

It's not always easy to be healthy. Here are some ways to be healthy and feel good.

Exercise

Doctors say it's important to exercise for thirty minutes a day, three days a week.

Eat healthy food

Don't forget to eat fruit and vegetables. They're good for you, and they taste good.

Have regular checkups

See your doctor for a checkup once a year. Always follow your doctor's health instructions.

If you feel sick, you can take over-the-counter medicine. Sometimes over-the-counter medicine helps people feel better. It's important to read and follow the directions exactly.[1] Over-the-counter medicines don't always stop the problem. Then, you have to go to the doctor.

[1]exactly = with no mistakes

B **Listen and read the article again.**

☑ Identify preventive care (CLB 3 L/R)
☑ Interpret medicine labels (CLB 3 R)
108 ☑ Copy medicine labels (CLB 2 W)

C **Circle the correct words.**

1. It's important to have a checkup every (month /(year)).
2. Eat (fruit and vegetables / over-the-counter medicine) every day.
3. It's important to exercise (three / thirty) days a week.
4. Always (feel / follow) the directions with over-the-counter medicine.

D **Complete the sentences. Use the words in the box.**

checkup	~~feel~~	exactly	healthy

1. Over-the-counter medicine can help you _____*feel*_____ better.
2. It's a good idea to go to the doctor for a _____ every year.
3. Follow all the directions _____ with over-the-counter medicine.
4. Exercise can help you be _____ and feel good.

3 Read directions and warnings on medicine labels

A **Look at the medicine labels. Match the sentences with the labels.**

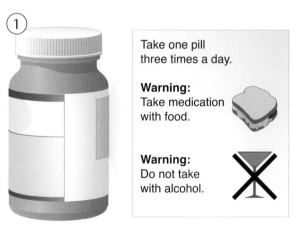

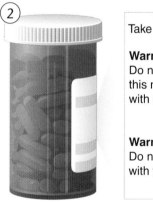

1. Do not take this with milk. __2__   4. Take this medicine twice a day. ____
2. Take this medicine with food. ____   5. Do not take this with food. ____
3. Do not take this with alcohol. ____   6. Take this medicine three times a day. ____

B **Think about the question. Talk about the answer with your class.**

What other warnings are on medicine labels? Name or draw 2 other warnings you know.

> **BRING IT TO LIFE**
>
> Go to a pharmacy. Look at a medicine label. Write the name of the medicine.
> Write or draw the directions and warnings in your notebook.

1 Grammar

A Circle the correct words.

1. The ((woman) / women) has a cold.
2. This (child / children) has to see the dentist.
3. Those (person / people) have to ride the bus.
4. His (teeth / tooth) hurts.
5. My (foot / feet) hurt.
6. The (man / men) have to talk to the nurse.

Grammar note

Irregular plural nouns

Singular	Plural
foot	feet
tooth	teeth
man	men
woman	women
child	children
person	people

B Match the questions with the answers.

__e__ 1. What's the matter with Maria?   a. He has to see the doctor.

____ 2. When does she have to leave?   b. No, he doesn't.

____ 3. Why does Carl have to leave early?   c. We leave early once a week.

____ 4. Does he leave early every day?   d. She has to leave at 2:00.

____ 5. How often do you leave early?   e. She has a backache.

C Write the questions.

1. _Does Rosa have to leave early?_ _____ Yes, she has to leave early.
2. _____ She has a stomach ache.
3. _____ She has to leave at 10:30.
4. _____ She has to go to the doctor.
5. _____ No, she doesn't always leave early.

D Complete the story. Use the words in the box.

~~is~~	have	at	isn't	has	on	receptionist	has to	wants

Today ____is____ Monday. Mr. Larson _____ an earache.
        1   2

He _____ see the doctor. He talks to the _____.
      3   4

The doctor doesn't _____ an opening today. There's an
                 5

opening _____ Tuesday _____ 10:00.
        6   7

Mr. Larson _____ happy. He _____ to see the doctor today.
          8   9

2 Group work

A Work with 2–3 classmates. Write 5 sentences about the picture on page 101. Talk about the sentences with your class.

A woman is sitting in the chair. She has an earache.

B Interview 3 classmates. Write their answers in your notebook.

ASK:

1. What do you have to do this afternoon?
2. How often do you have to clean the house?
3. Do you have to work this weekend?

Classmate—Rafik
1. go to the bank
2. once a week
3. yes

C Talk about the answers with your class.

PROBLEM SOLVING

A Listen and read about David. What is his problem?

David teaches English in the evening. He likes his job and his students very much. Every day he tells his students, "You have to come to school every day. Don't stay home! Come and learn English every day." David has a problem today. He has a terrible headache and a stomach ache, too. He doesn't want to go home, but he feels terrible.

B Work with your classmates. Answer the question. (More than one answer is possible.)

What can David do?
    a. Call the doctor.
    b. Go home now.
    c. Stay at school now, but stay home tomorrow.
    d. Other: _____

C Work with your classmates. What can David tell his students?

Getting the Job

FOCUS ON
Critical thinking:
- Interpret help-wanted ads
- Analyse and describe personal work experience
- Interpret a time card
- Describe ability or lack of ability

LESSON **1** Vocabulary

1 Learn names of jobs

A Look at the pictures. Point to the person cleaning a school.

B Listen and look at the pictures.

C Listen and repeat the words.

1. pharmacist   3. mechanic   5. server

2. homemaker   4. janitor   6. childcare worker

D Look at the pictures. Complete the sentences.

1. A _____mechanic_____ works in a garage.

2. A _____ works at home.

3. A _____ works in a childcare centre.

4. A _____ works at a school.

5. A _____ works in a pharmacy.

6. A _____ works in a restaurant.

☑ Identify job titles and job skills (CLB 2 L/R)
☑ Copy information (CLB 1 W)
112 ☑ Describe jobs and skills (CLB 2, 3 W)

2 Talk about jobs and skills

A Work with your classmates. Match the words with the picture.

_____ bus person   _1_ delivery person   _____ manager   _____ plumber

_____ cook   _____ gardener   _____ painter   _____ server

B Listen and check your answers. Then practise the words with a partner.

C Complete the sentences.

1. A ___plumber___ fixes sinks.

2. A _____ cleans tables.

3. A _____ works in gardens.

4. A _____ cooks food.

5. A _____ delivers packages.

6. A _____ manages a business.

7. A _____ serves food.

8. A _____ paints buildings.

D Work with a partner. Ask and answer questions about jobs. Use the picture in 2A.

A: Who is he?

B: He's a cook.

A: What's he doing?

B: He's cooking.

TEST YOURSELF ✔

Close your book. Write 5 jobs and 5 job skills. Check your spelling in a dictionary.

1 Read about getting a job

A Look at the pictures. Listen.

B Listen again. Read the sentences.

1. Sergei was a pharmacist in Russia. Now he lives in Toronto.
2. He's looking for a job.
3. He looks at the help-wanted ads in the newspaper.
4. He sees a sign in a pet store window and applies for the job.
5. He has an interview and gets the job.
6. Sergei is happy. He loves his new job.

C Check your understanding. Mark the sentences T (true) or F (false).

__F__ 1. Sergei lives in Russia now.

_____ 2. He is a pharmacist in Toronto.

_____ 3. He looks in the newspaper for a job.

_____ 4. He sees a sign on the Internet.

_____ 5. He gets a job.

_____ 6. He loves his job.

2 Write about looking for a job

A Write about how to look for a job. Complete the sentences.

Are you looking for a job?

You can look _____ or look

_____ to find a job.

Then, you _____ and

have an _____. Good luck!

Need help?

You can look...

in the newspaper.
in store windows.
on the Internet.

B Read your sentences to a partner.

☑ Identify ways to find a job (CLB 2 L/R)
☑ Interpret job ads (CLB 2 R)
114 ☑ Describe ways to find a job (CLB 2, 3 W)

3 Read help-wanted ads

A Look at the help-wanted ads. Read about the jobs.

1.
HELP WANTED
Driver
Evenings, part-time
(18 hours a week)
Call Tom.
(647) 829-3025

2.
Mechanic Needed
FT (40 hours a week)
See Bill.
Southside Auto Repair
9245 Clark Avenue

3.
Manager Needed
Full-time
Apply at Pizza King.
227 Main Street

4.
HELP WANTED
Cleaning staff
PT (25 hours a week),
late nights
Call Carla for an application.
(613) 565-2074

B Look at the help-wanted ads again. Read the sentences.
Check (✔) the correct boxes.

	Job #1	Job #2	Job #3	Job #4
1. This job is part-time (PT).	✔			✔
2. This job is full-time (FT).				
3. This job is on Main Street.				
4. This job is in the evenings.				
5. You have to talk to Bill for this job.				
6. You have to talk to Carla for this job.				

C Work with a partner. Ask and answer questions about the help-wanted ads in 3A.

1. What's the job?
2. Is it part-time or full-time?
3. How many hours is the job?
4. Who can I talk to about the job?

TEST YOURSELF ✔

Close your book. Write a help-wanted ad for a job you want. Share your ad with a partner.

1 Learn the simple past with *be*

A Look at the pictures. Was Rico a student or a gardener in 1992?

farmer 1980–1991   student 1991–1993   gardener 1994–2002   business owner 2002–present

B Study the charts. Complete the sentences below.

THE SIMPLE PAST WITH *BE*

Statements					
I	was	a gardener.	We	were	gardeners.
You	were		You		
He She	was		They		

1. He _____ a gardener.   2. They _____ gardeners.

Negative statements					
I	was not	a gardener.	We	were not	gardeners.
You	were not		You		
He She	was not		They		

Contractions

was not = wasn't
  I wasn't a gardener.
were not = weren't
  They weren't gardeners.

3. He _____ a gardener.   4. We _____ gardeners.

C Complete the sentences. Use the information in 1A.

1. Rico _____was_____ a farmer in 1980.

2. Rico and his brothers _____ gardeners in 1994.

3. They _____ gardeners in 1981.

4. Rico _____ a student in 2001.

116   ☑ Describe work experience (CLB 2 S/W)

2 Ask and answer *Yes/No* questions

A Study the chart. Ask and answer the questions.

Yes/No questions and answers	
A: Were you a doctor ten years ago? **B:** Yes, I was. *or* No, I wasn't.	**A:** Were you at home last night? **B:** Yes, we were. *or* No, we weren't.
A: Was he a student five months ago? **B:** Yes, he was. *or* No, he wasn't.	**A:** Were they at school last week? **B:** Yes, they were. *or* No, they weren't.

B Match the questions with the answers.

_c_ 1. Were they at home yesterday?   a. Yes, he was.

____ 2. Was she a student in Brazil?   b. No, I wasn't.

____ 3. Were you a student six years ago?   c. No, they weren't.

____ 4. Was he at school last week?   d. Yes, she was.

C Complete the questions. Then write the answers.

1. __Was__ Rico a farmer 25 years ago? _Yes, he was._____

2. _____ Rico a student last year?   _____

3. _____ you a student in 2004?   _____

4. _____ you at school yesterday?   _____

3 Practise *Yes/No* questions

A Complete the questions with a job. Write your answers.

1. In your home country, were you (a) / an ____gardener____? _____

2. In your home country, were you a / an _____? _____

3. In your home country, were you a / an _____? _____

B Ask and answer the questions in 3A with a partner. Then write sentences about your partner's answers.

Jinhee was a gardener in South Korea.

TEST YOURSELF ✔

Close your book. Write 2 to 4 sentences about your work experience.

I was a homemaker from 1990 to 1998. I was a server from 1998 to 2002.

1 Learn about a job interview

A Read Isabel Monte's job application. Match the questions with the answers.

Applicant name: Isabel Monte	Position: Office Assistant
Experience:	Skills: use a computer, make copies,
Receptionist 2005-present Vancouver	answer phones, speak English and Spanish
Office Manager 1995-2005 Santa Ana	Education: English classes,
Office Assistant 1988-1996 Santa Ana	computer classes, business classes

__d__ 1. When was Isabel an office manager?   a. Santa Ana

____ 2. Does she have office skills?   b. office assistant

____ 3. Where was she in 1998?   c. yes

____ 4. What job does she want?   d. from 1995 to 2005

B Listen and read.

A: Tell me about yourself, Mr. Tran.

B: I'm from Vietnam. I lived there for thirty years.

A: Do you have work experience?

B: Yes, I do. I was a restaurant manager for two years.
I can cook, serve food, and wash dishes, too.

A: Can you work weekends?

B: Yes, I can.

A: That's great. You're hired!

C Listen again and repeat.

D Work with a partner. Practise the conversation. Use
your own information.

A: Tell me about yourself, _____.

B: I'm from _____. I lived there
for _____ years.

A: Do you have work experience?

B: Yes, I do. I was a _____ for _____ years.
I can _____ and _____.

A: That's great. You're hired!

> **Need help?**
>
> **A:** Do you have work
> experience?
> **B:** Yes, I do. *or*
> No, I don't, but I can
> learn quickly.

E Listen and match the people with the job skills.

_____ 1. Gladys   a. He can fix sinks and toilets.

_____ 2. Ken   b. She can help patients.

_____ 3. Franco   c. He can fill prescriptions.

_____ 4. Molly   d. She can cook, clean, pay bills, and take care of children.

2 Learn questions with *can*

A Study the chart. Complete the sentences below.

Questions with *can*		
Can	you he she they	fix cars?

Answers						
Yes,	I he she they	can.	No,	I he she they	can't.

1. A: Can he _____ cars?

    B: Yes, he _____ .

2. A: _____ he fix sinks?

    B: No, he _____ .

B Work with a partner. Ask and answer questions with *can*.

A: Can you fix cars?

B: Yes, I can.

A: Can you manage a restaurant?

B: No, I can't.

3 Practise your pronunciation

A Listen and repeat.

Can	Can't
I can ride a bicycle.	I can't drive a bus.
Jose can speak English.	He can't speak Chinese.

B Listen for *can* or *can't*. Circle *a* or *b*.

1. a. can   (b.) can't   3. a. can   b. can't   5. a. can   b. can't

2. a. can   b. can't   4. a. can   b. can't   6. a. can   b. can't

TEST YOURSELF ✔

Work with a partner. Tell a partner about 3 job skills you have. Then change roles.

I can fix sinks, I can speak English and Chinese, and I can drive a truck.

FOCUS ON

Socio-cultural competence:
• Sensitivity to register
Real-life math
• Calculate pay based on time card information

1 Get ready to read

A **Read the definitions.**

employee: worker

boss: the person you work for; your supervisor or manager

co-workers: people who work with you; other employees

B **Work with your classmates. Which questions can you ask your boss? Which questions can you ask your co-workers?**

1. Can I leave early today?
2. How do I use the photocopier?
3. Do you like your job here?
4. Where's the lunchroom?

2 Read about great employees

A **Read the quiz. Then answer the questions.**

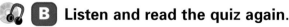

Are You Good or Are You Great?

Are you a good employee, or a great employee? Check (✔) *yes* or *no* for each sentence.
Then count the number of *yes* answers you have. Read what your answers say about you.

1 I always read memos[1] and employee information from my boss.

Yes _____ No _____

2 I ask my co-workers for help or advice.

Yes _____ No _____

3 I come to work on time or a little early every day.

Yes _____ No _____

4 I call my boss on days I can't come to work.

Yes _____ No _____

5 I complete my time card on time.

Yes _____ No _____

What your answers say about you:
5 yes answers: You are an excellent employee!
3–4 yes answers: You are working hard. You're a good employee!
1–2 yes answers: Need help? Ask a co-worker. You can learn something new every day.

[1]memo: a note from a boss to the employee(s)

B **Listen and read the quiz again.**

☑ Identify appropriate workplace behaviour (CLB 3, 4 L/S)
☑ Interpret a time card (CLB 2 R)
☑ Interpret quizzes (CLB 3, 4 R)

C **Complete the sentences. Circle *a* or *b*.**

1. Ask your co-workers for ____ .
   a. help   b. memos

2. A memo is usually from the ____ .
   a. employees   b. boss

3. Call your ____ on days you can't work.
   a. co-worker   b. boss

4. Come to work ____ .
   a. on time   b. sometimes

3 Read a time card

A **Look at the time card. Complete the sentences.**

Quick Stop Car Wash	**Employee Time Card**		
Name: **White, Joey**	Employee number: **0521**	Rate: **$12.50**	Pay Period: **June 1–June 7**

Day	Time in	Time out	Hours
Monday	8:00 a.m.	2:00 p.m.	6
Wednesday	8:00 a.m.	2:00 p.m.	6
Friday	8:00 a.m.	2:00 p.m.	6
Total hours:			18

1. A pay period at Quick Stop Car Wash is _____ days.

2. Joey was at work on _____ , _____ and _____ .

3. Joey was at work from _____ to _____ on Monday.

B **Think about the questions. Talk about the answers with your class.**

1. Is the rate of pay at Quick Stop Car Wash good?
2. Is Joey's work schedule a good work schedule for you? Why or why not?

4 Real-life math

Look at Joey's time card again. Answer the questions.

Joey works the same schedule every week.

1. How much money does he make every pay period? _____

2. How much money does he make in a year? _____

> **BRING IT TO LIFE**
>
> Find magazine pictures of employees and bosses at work. Bring the pictures to class. Talk about the pictures with your classmates.
>
> Find job ads on the Internet and in the newspaper that match your skills. Present the details (skills, qualifications, salary) to your class.

1 Grammar

A **Complete the sentences with *can* or *can't*.**

1. I can speak English,
   and Henry _____can_____, too.

2. My son can cook,
   but my daughter _____.

3. I can take care of children,
   and Jackie _____, too.

4. I can fix sinks, and I _____ fix bathtubs, too.

5. David _____ speak English, but he can't speak Italian.

6. Bill can help patients, but he _____ manage a restaurant.

Grammar note

and/too
   I can cook. Mary can cook.
   I can cook, **and** Mary can, too.
but
   I can cook. Tom can't cook.
   I can cook, **but** Tom can't.

B **Complete the questions and answers. Use *was, wasn't, were,* or *weren't*.**

1. _Was_____ Mei a doctor in China?   Yes, she _____was_____.

2. _____ they in Hong Kong last month?   No, they _____.

3. _____ Mr. Morris at work yesterday?   No, he _____.

4. _____ you at home last Monday?   No, we _____.

5. _____ the girls in Winnipeg two weeks ago?   Yes, they _____.

C **Match the questions and answers.**

__c_ 1. Where were Tad and Elena yesterday?   a. He was a mechanic.

____ 2. Was Elena a plumber in Toronto?   b. Julio and Elda were their friends.

____ 3. What was Tad's job five years ago?   c. They were at school.

____ 4. Who were their friends in Chile?   d. They were students in 2005.

____ 5. When were they students?   e. No, she wasn't.

D **Complete the story. Circle the correct words.**

Hector is (for / (from)) Brazil. He (lived / doesn't) there for forty years. He (was / were) a
             1   2   3

teacher in Brazil. He (was / can) teach math and computers. Hector (live / lives) in British
                 4   5

Columbia now. He wants to teach, (but / ago) now he's studying English. He goes to
                                      6

English class (twice / three) times a week. His class in on Mondays, Wednesdays,
                   7

(and / but) Fridays.
   8

2 Group work

A Work with 2–3 classmates. Choose 3 people from the picture on page 113. Write 2 sentences about each person's work experience. Talk about the sentences with your class.

The cook was a restaurant manager in Greece.
He can cook, serve food, and manage a restaurant.

B Interview 3 classmates. Write their answers in your notebook.

ASK:

1. What was your job in your home country?
2. Do you have a job now?
3. Are you looking for a new job?

C Talk about the answers with your class.

> Classmate—Wen
> 1. He was a teacher.
> 2. No, he doesn't.
> 3. Yes, he is.

PROBLEM SOLVING

A Listen and read about Mrs. Galvan. What is her problem?

Mrs. Galvan moved to Victoria this week. She's looking for a job. She can work weekdays, but she can't work on weekends. Mrs. Galvan was a restaurant manager in Vancouver. She can use a computer, cook, and serve food. Mrs. Galvan is worried. She needs to start work this week.

Food Server
PT, M–F 9:00–2:00
$8 per hour

Restaurant Manager
Nights and weekends
$18 per hour

Assistant Manager
FT, M–F 8:30 a.m.–4:30 p.m.
$12 per hour

B Work with your classmates. Look at the job ads and answer the question. (More than one answer is possible.)

What is the best job for Mrs. Galvan?

C Work with your classmates. Make a list of other jobs Mrs. Galvan can do.

FOCUS ON

Critical thinking:
- Interpret traffic signs
- Classify behaviour as safe or unsafe
- Classify language learning habits as positive or negative
- Describe emergencies to a 911 operator
- Interpret a pie chart of accident data

LESSON 1   Vocabulary

1   Learn traffic signs

A   Look at the pictures. What colours, numbers, and words do you see?

B   Listen and look at the pictures.

①    ②    ③

④    ⑤    ⑥

C   Listen and repeat the words.

1. stop	3. school crossing	5. no left turn
2. road work	4. no parking	6. speed limit

D   Look at the pictures. Complete the sentences.

1. The _____ no left turn _____ sign with the black arrow means you can't turn left.
2. There's a yellow _____ sign. Students can walk here.
3. The sign with the number gives the _____. Drive 50 kilometres per hour here.
4. There's a red _____ sign. You have to stop.
5. There's an orange _____ sign. People are working on the street.
6. The _____ sign with the "P" means you can't park here.

☑ Identify traffic signs and workplace safety equipment (CLB 2 L/R)

124 ☑ Describe traffic signs and workplace safety equipment (CLB 3 W)

2 Talk about work safety

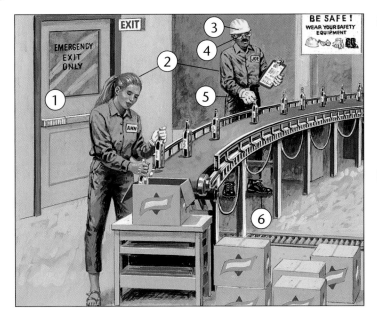

A Work with your classmates. Match the words with the pictures.

____ careful	____ factory workers	____ safety boots
____ careless	____ fire extinguisher	____ safety glasses
____ dangerous/unsafe	____ hard hat	____ safety gloves
_1_ emergency exit	____ safe	____ wet floor

B Listen and check your answers. Then practise the words with a partner.

C Look at the factory workers. Match the names with the descriptions.

_b_ 1. Ann   a. He's careless. He doesn't see the wet floor.

____ 2. Joe   b. She's careless. She isn't wearing her safety boots.

____ 3. Tim   c. She's careful. She wears safety glasses and safety gloves.

____ 4. Tanya   d. He's careful. He's wearing safety glasses and safety gloves.

D Work with a partner. Ask and answer questions.
Talk about the factory workers in 2A.

A: Is Tanya careful or careless at work?

B: She's careful. She wears a hard hat. How about Tim?

A: He's careless. He doesn't wear safety boots.

TEST YOURSELF ✔

Close your book. Write 6 words for traffic signs and 4 words for safety equipment. Check your spelling in a dictionary.

1 Read about safe and dangerous behaviour

A Look at the pictures. Listen.

B Listen again. Read the sentences.

1. I always drive fast. I never wear a seat belt. My friends worry, but I don't.
2. I always talk on my cell phone at work.
3. My co-workers say I should be careful, but I don't worry.
4. I never check the smoke detectors at home. My sister worries, but I don't.
5. My sister, my friends, and my co-workers worry too much. They should relax.
6. Oh, no! Here comes a police officer. Maybe I should worry now.

C Check your understanding. Circle the correct words.

1. Frank ((drives) / doesn't drive) fast.
2. His friends (worry / don't worry).
3. Frank likes his (couch / cell phone).
4. Frank isn't (careful / careless).

2 Write about your behaviour

A Write your story. Complete the sentences.

I _____ drive fast.

I _____ wear a seat belt.

I _____ talk on a cell phone at work or in the car.

I _____ check my smoke detector at home.

Need help?

Adverbs of frequency
always
usually
sometimes
never

B Read your story to a partner.

☑ Interpret and identify safe and unsafe behaviour (CLB 2 L/R)
126 ☑ Describe safety habits (CLB 3 S/W)

3 Make a safety checklist

A Listen and complete the questions.
Then check (✔) *Yes, I do.* or *No, I don't.*

Do you...	Yes, I do.	No, I don't.
1. always drive the ___speed limit___ ?	✔	
2. drive fast near _____?		
3. know where the emergency _____ are in the building?		
4. wear _____ equipment at work?		
5. have a _____ detector in the kitchen?		

Are you safe?

B Work with a partner. Talk about your safety habits at home, at work, and in the car. Use the chart.

A: *Do you wear safety equipment at work?*
B: *Yes, I always wear safety equipment. Do you?*

4 Real-life math

Read about the workers. Answer the questions.

Twenty-five of the one hundred workers at ABC Chemical Factory never wear their safety gloves. That means 25% never wear their gloves and 75% wear them.

Ten of the one hundred workers never wear their safety glasses.

1. What percent of the workers don't wear their safety glasses? _____%

2. What percent of the workers wear their safety glasses? _____%

Some workers at ABC Chemical Factory

TEST YOURSELF ✓

Close your book. Write 3 things you do to be safe at home, in the car, or at work. Talk about your ideas with the class.

1 Learn *should* and *should not*

A Look at the poster. Read the sentences. How can people be safe at home?

You should:	You should NOT:
Know your neighbours. Lock doors and windows at night. Tell the manager about problems.	Open the door to strangers. Leave the building door open. Walk alone in the parking lot at night.

B Study the charts. Complete the sentences below.

SHOULD AND *SHOULD NOT*

Statements					
I You He She	should	lock the door.	We You They	should	lock the door.

1. He _____ lock the door.   2. We should _____ the door.

Negative statements						Contractions
I You He She	should not	walk alone.	We You They	should not	walk alone.	should not = shouldn't You shouldn't walk alone.

3. She _____ walk alone.   4. They _____ alone.

C Complete the sentences with *should* or *shouldn't*. Use the poster in 1A. Read the sentences to a partner.

1. You _____*shouldn't*_____ leave the front door open.

2. You _____ walk in the parking lot with other people.

3. You _____ close the building door.

4. You _____ open the door to strangers.

2 Ask and answer information questions with *should*

A Study the chart. Ask and answer the questions.

Information questions and answers with *should*	
A: When should she walk with a friend? **B:** She should walk with a friend at night.	**A:** What should they do? **B:** They should lock the door.

B Match the questions with the answers.

_b_ 1. Sara has to walk home at night. What should she do?

_____ 2. I don't understand. What should I do?

_____ 3. Bob has a toothache. Where should he go?

_____ 4. We are students. When should we study?

_____ 5. Jen has a fever. What should she do?

a. We should study every day.

b. She should walk with a friend.

c. You should ask for help.

d. She should call the doctor.

e. He should go to the dentist.

3 Use *should* to talk about classroom rules

A Work with a partner. Answer the question.
What should students do in class?

B Work with a partner. Complete the poster below with the rules of your class.

Follow Classroom Rules! It's Easy!

Students should . . .	Students shouldn't . . .
1. speak English in class.	4. sleep in class.
2. _____.	5. _____.
3. _____.	6. _____.

TEST YOURSELF ✔

Close your book. Write 3 sentences about your school's safety rules.
Use *should* or *shouldn't*.

1 Learn to call 911

A Look at the pictures. Then answer the questions.

1

There's a traffic accident.

2

There's a robbery.

3

There's a fire.

296 GREEN STREET

1. Who needs help?

_____

2. What's the emergency?

_____

3. Where's the emergency?

_____

B Listen and read.

A: 911. Emergency.
B: There's a fire at my neighbour's house.
A: What's the address?
B: It's 412 Oak Street.
A: Is anyone hurt?
B: I don't know.
A: OK. Help is on the way.

Is anyone hurt?

I don't know.

C Listen again and repeat.

D Work with a partner. Practise the conversation. Use emergencies from 1A.

A: 911. Emergency.
B: _____.
A: What's the address?
B: It's _____.
A: Is anyone hurt?
B: _____.
A: OK. _____ is on the way.

> **Need help?**
>
> **Help** is on the way.
> **A police officer** is on the way.
> **An ambulance** is on the way.
>
>

✔ Ask for assistance in an emergency phone call (CLB 3, 4 L/S)

E Listen and write the emergency information.

1. What: <u>car accident</u>
   Where: <u>Pine Ave. and Hope St.</u>
   Who needs help: <u>a man</u>

2. What: _____
   Where: _____
   Who needs help: _____

3. What: _____
   Where: _____
   Who needs help: _____

4. What: _____
   Where: _____
   Who needs help: _____

2 Practise your pronunciation

A Listen and point to the word you hear.

should   shouldn't

B Listen for _should_ or _shouldn't_. Circle _a_ or _b_.

1. a. should
   (b.) shouldn't

2. a. should
   b. shouldn't

3. a. should
   b. shouldn't

4. a. should
   b. shouldn't

5. a. should
   b. shouldn't

6. a. should
   b. shouldn't

C Work with a partner. Read the sentences. Should you call 911? Check (✔) the correct boxes.

A: _I have a headache._
B: _You shouldn't call 911._

	Should	Shouldn't
1. I have a headache.		✔
2. My friend has a stomach ache.		
3. There's a fire in the kitchen.		
4. I need a prescription.		
5. There's a bad car accident.		
6. There's a robbery.		

TEST YOURSELF ✔

Work with a partner. Partner A: Report an emergency. Partner B:
Ask for more information. Tell your partner that help is on the way.
Then change roles.

1 Get ready to read

A Read the definitions.

pull over: to drive the car to the side of the road and stop in a safe place

cause: to make something happen

pull over

B Work with your classmates. Ask and answer the questions.

1. Why do people have car accidents?
2. Why do people pull over?

2 Read about safe drivers

A Read the article.

Safe Driving Tips

Canada has one of the best road safety records in the world. Each year, approximately 2,900 people are killed and more than 220,000 are injured on Canadian roads.

- Wear your seatbelt. Whether you're a driver or passenger, buckle up.[1]
- Don't drink and drive.
- If you're tired, pull over to the side of the road.
- Turn your cell phone off before you start driving. Let callers leave a message.
- Check local weather and road conditions before leaving your home. Bring a map and be prepared to take an alternative route.

[1]buckle up – fasten your seatbelt

Source: *Transport Canada*

B Listen and read the article again.

☑ Describe the traffic in your neighbourhood (CLB 3, 4 S)
☑ Interpret traffic safety and accident prevention tips (CLB 3, 4 L/R)
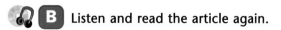

C Complete the sentences. Use the words in the box.

read a map	pull over	cell phone	speeding	~~pay attention~~

1. You should ____pay attention____ when you are driving a car.
2. You shouldn't _____ when you are driving.
3. You have to _____ if you have an accident.
4. You should pull over to use a _____.
5. _____ causes 20% of traffic accidents.

D Read and check (✔) *yes* or *no*.

Should you pull over...	Yes	No
1. when you are tired?	✔	
2. when you see a stop sign?		
3. when you see a road work sign?		
4. when you have to read a map?		
5. when you have to use your cell phone?		
6. when you have an accident?		

3 Learn about traffic accidents

A Look at the pie chart. Complete the sentences.

In 2005:

1. _53.3%_ of drivers lost their lives.
2. The percentage of passengers who died was _____.
3. _____ of pedestrians died because of accidents.
4. The percentage of motorcyclists who had fatal accidents was _____.
5. _____ of bicyclists lost their lives because of unsafe roads.

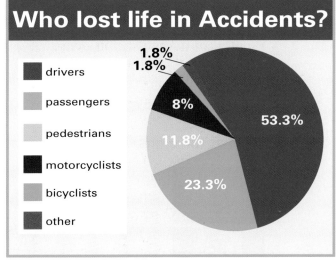

Source: *Transport Canada*

B Think about the statistics. Talk about them with your class.

What can cause accidents?

> **BRING IT TO LIFE**
>
> Watch the traffic in your neighbourhood. Are the drivers paying attention?
> Tell your classmates about the drivers in your neighbourhood.

FOCUS ON

Socio-cultural competence/
problem solving:
• Determine appropriate
  behaviour following an accident

1 Grammar

A Write the answers to the questions.

1. There's a school crossing sign. Should I slow down?
   <u>Yes, you should.</u>

2. Teo is driving to work. Should he wear his seat belt?
   _____

3. The floor is wet. Should Min and Janet walk on it?
   _____

4. I'm driving home, but I'm very tired. Should I pull over?
   _____

Grammar note

**Yes/No questions
with should**

A: Should I call 911?
B: Yes, you should. *or*
   No, you shouldn't.

A: Should he wear gloves?
B: Yes, he should. *or*
   No, he shouldn't.

B Match the questions with the answers.

<u>c</u> 1. What's the emergency?   a. A man and a woman.

____ 2. What should I do?   b. 122 Pine Street.

____ 3. Who needs help?   c. There's a car accident.

____ 4. Where's the emergency?   d. No, they shouldn't.

____ 5. Should people drink and drive? e. You should call 911.

C Put the conversation in order.

____ It's 2386 3rd Avenue.   <u>1</u> 911. Emergency.   ____ What's the address?

____ Help is on the way.   ____ There's a fire.

D Look at the signs. Read the sentences. Write your advice.

1. Luis isn't paying attention.
   <u>He should watch for children.</u>

2. Anne is looking for a place to park.
   _____

3. Ted is driving sixty-five kilometres per hour.
   _____

4. Molly is driving and talking to her friend.
   _____

2 Group work

A Work with 2–3 classmates. Look at the pictures on page 125.
Write 5 sentences with *should* or *shouldn't*.
Talk about the sentences with your class.

Ann should wear safety glasses. Tim shouldn't listen to music at work.

B Interview 3 classmates. Write their answers in your notebook.

ASK:
1. How often do you wear your seat belt?
2. Do you check your smoke detector batteries every 6 months?
3. How often do you wear safety glasses or gloves?

> Classmate—Lina
> 1. She always wears her seat belt.
> 2. Yes, she does.
> 3. She sometimes wears safety glasses.

C Talk about the answers with your class.

PROBLEM SOLVING

A Listen and read about Mr. Brown. What is his problem?

Mr. Brown is in the parking lot at the supermarket. He's very tired. He's parking his car and he doesn't see the car next to him! He has a small accident. He looks around the parking lot, but the driver of the other car is not there.

B Work with your classmates. Answer the question.
(More than one answer is possible.)

What should Mr. Brown do?
    a. Call the police.
    b. Call 911.
    c. Talk to the store manager.
    d. Other: _____

C Work with your classmates. Write a note that Mr. Brown can put on the car for the driver.

UNIT **12**

FOCUS ON
_____

Critical thinking:
• Classify leisure activities by season
• Interpret information on a bus schedule
• Interpret information from a phone book

Free Time

LESSON 1 Vocabulary

1 Learn weather words and holidays

A Look at the pictures. When are the holidays?

B Listen and look at the pictures.

C Listen and repeat the words.

1. snowing   2. cloudy   3. sunny   4. hot   5. raining   6. cold

D Look at the pictures. Complete the sentences.

1. It's _____hot_____ this Canada Day.
2. It's _____ this Thanksgiving.
3. It's _____ this Father's Day.

4. It's _____ this New Year's Day.
5. It's _____ this Mother's Day.
6. It's _____ this Labour Day.

☑ Identify and discuss weather conditions and Canadian holidays (CLB 1 L/R)

136 ☑ Describe favourite activities (CLB 1 W)

2 Talk about leisure activities

A **Work with your classmates. Match the words with the pictures.**

_____ go out to eat	_____ go to the movies	_____ play soccer
_____ go swimming	_____ have a picnic	_1_ stay home
_____ go to the beach	_____ make a snowman	

B **Listen and check your answers. Then practise the words with a partner.**

C **Look at the pictures. Circle the correct words.**

1. In the winter, it's ((cold) / hot). They like to (play soccer / (stay home)).
2. The flowers are beautiful in the (fall / spring). They like to have (movies / picnics).
3. The weather is (hot / cold) in the summer. They like to (go / stay) to the beach.
4. In the fall, they like to go (out to eat / to the beach). Other people like to go (swimming / to the movies).

D **Work with a partner. Ask and answer the questions.**

1. What is your favourite time of the year?
2. What do you like to do at that time of the year?

TEST YOURSELF ✓

Close your book. Write your 5 favourite activities for hot and cold weather.
Check your spelling in a dictionary.

FOCUS ON

Socio-cultural competence:
• Hockey culture; the role of sports in social interactions
Functional competence:
• Requesting information

1 Read about a trip to a hockey game

A Look at the pictures. Listen.

B Listen again. Read the sentences.

1. I can't wait for the weekend. I don't have to work or go to school on Saturdays or Sundays.
2. On Saturdays, I have fun with my son.
3. This Saturday, we're going to see a hockey game.
4. We're going to watch the game and eat hot dogs.
5. My son wants to sit behind the bench at the game.

C Check your understanding. Circle *a* or *b*.

1. He _____ on Saturday.

   a. works

   b. doesn't work

2. They're going to see a hockey game _____.

   a. on Saturday

   b. on Sunday

3. He's going to see the game with his _____.

   a. boss

   b. son

4. His son wants to sit behind the _____ at the game.

   a. puck

   b. bench

☑ Identify leisure activities (CLB 2 L/R)
☑ Identify and respond to requests (CLB 2 S/L)
☑ Interpret bus schedule (CLB 2 R)
138 ☑ Describe leisure activities (CLB 2 W)

2 Write about your plans

A Write your story. Complete the sentences.

I can't wait for _____.

I don't _____ on _____.

On _____, I'm going to _____.

B Read your story to a partner.

3 Use a bus schedule to plan a trip

A Listen to the conversation. Complete the schedule below.

	Grant Street	Front St. School	Town Mall	Riverside Hockey Arena	City Park
Bus #1	_8:00_	8:15	_____	8:45	9:00
Bus #2	12:00	_____	12:30	12:45	_____
Bus #3	4:00	4:15	4:30	_____	5:00

Metro Bus West Line–Weekend Schedule

B Match the questions with the answers.

Pedro and his son have to get on the bus at Grant Street. The hockey game is at 1:00.

_b_ 1. What bus do they have to take?   a. 12:45

____ 2. How many stops are between Grant Street and the arena?   b. Bus #2

____ 3. What time do they have to take the bus?   c. two

____ 4. What time will they stop at the arena?   d. 12:00

C Work with a partner. Practise the conversation. Use the bus schedule in 3A.

You are on Grant Street.

A: Excuse me, I have to be at the mall at 5:00.
    Can I take the bus from here?

B: Yes. Take the number 3 bus at 4:00.

A: Thank you.

1 Learn the future with *be going to*

A Look at the pictures. What season is it?

It's going to be sunny on Friday.

It's going to be cloudy on Saturday.

It's going to rain on Sunday.

B Study the charts. Complete the sentences below.

THE FUTURE WITH *BE GOING TO*

Statements							
I	am			We			
You	are	going to	have a picnic.	You	are	going to	have a picnic.
He She	is			They			
It	is	going to	be sunny.				

1. She is _____ have a picnic.

2. They _____ going _____ have a picnic.

Negative statements							
I	am			We			
You	are	not going to	have a picnic.	You	are	not going to	have a picnic.
He She	is			They			
It	is	not going to	be sunny.				

3. I am _____ going to have a picnic.

4. We are not _____ have a picnic.

C Look at the pictures in 1A. Match the parts of the sentences.

_b_ 1. They are going to   a. rain on Saturday.

____ 2. It is going to   b. have a picnic on Friday.

____ 3. They are not going to   c. stay home on Saturday.

____ 4. It is not going to   d. rain on Sunday.

2 Ask and answer questions with *be going to*

A Study the chart. Ask and answer the questions.

Information questions with *be going to*	
A: What are you going to do tonight? **B:** I'm going to study.	**A:** What are we going to do next week? **B:** We're going to (go to) Mexico.
A: What is he going to do tomorrow? **B:** He's going to see a movie.	**A:** What are they going to do next year? **B:** They're going to buy a house.

B Write the questions.

1. _What is she going to do tonight?_ She's going to watch TV tonight.
2. _____ I'm going to have a picnic on Saturday.
3. _____ We're going to have fun this weekend.
4. _____ They're going to study tomorrow.
5. _____ He's going to feed the dog tonight.

3 Practise questions with *be going to*

A Complete the questions. Use the words in the box. Then write your answers.

What   Who   When   ~~Where~~

1. _Where_____ are you going to go after class?

   _I'm going to go home._____

2. _____ are you going to do tomorrow?

   _____

3. _____ are you going to see a movie?

   _____

4. _____ are you going to talk to after class?

   _____

B Ask and answer the questions in 3A with a partner. Then write sentences about your partner's answers.

Igor is going to go to work.

⌐ **TEST YOURSELF** ✔ ⌐

Close your book. Write 2 sentences about your future plans and 2 sentences about your partner's future plans.

I'm going to study tomorrow. Igor is going to go to work.

LESSON 4 **Everyday conversation**

FOCUS ON
_____
Real-life math:
• Calculate times in order to
  make plans

1 Plan to see a movie

A Read the movie ads. Say the titles and the times of the movies.

TOWN MALL THEATRE

Where's the MONEY? **PG**
Times: 5:30*, 8:00
Running Time: 90 minutes
$12.50 Adults $8.00 Children

THE ACTION MAN PG-13
Times: 6:00*, 8:45
Running Time: 120 minutes
$12.50 Adults $8.00 Children

RAIN IN MY EYES R
Times: 9:30
Running Time: 120 minutes
$12.50 Adults

My Friend **GREEN GEORGE** *Family night special!* G
Times: 4:00*, 6:00*, 7:30
Running Time: 75 minutes
$12.50 Adults $8.00 Children

Bargain matinee show times 4:00–6:30. All tickets $8.00.

B Listen and read.

A: What are we going to do tonight?

B: Let's see a movie. *The Action Man* is playing at 6:00.

A: OK. How much are tickets?

B: The 6:00 show is only $8.00.

A: $8.00? That's a bargain. Let's go!

C Listen again and repeat.

D Work with a partner. Practise the conversation. Use the movie ads in 1A.

A: What are we _____ do tonight?

B: _____ see a movie? _____ is playing at _____.

A: Sure. How much are _____?

B: _____.

A: _____? Let's go!

E Listen to the conversation. Answer the questions.

1. What movie are they going to see? _____Rain in My Eyes_____

2. What time are they going to meet? _____

3. What time is the movie? _____

4. Can they take the bus? _____

☑ Interpret information about movies (CLB 3 R)

142 ☑ Describe plans to see a movie (CLB 3 L/S)

2 Practise your pronunciation

 A **Listen to the sentences. What is different in the "relaxed" pronunciation?**

	Formal	Relaxed
1. going to	A: What are we **going to** do today? B: We're **going to** go to the park.	A: What are we **going to** do today? B: We're **going to** go to the park.
2. want to	A: Do you **want to** go to a movie? B: Yes. I **want to** go to a movie.	A: Do you **want to** go to a movie? B: Yes. I **want to** go to a movie.

 B **Listen and circle** *formal* **or** *relaxed*.

1. (formal)   relaxed
2. formal   relaxed
3. formal   relaxed
4. formal   relaxed
5. formal   relaxed

C **Work with a partner. Read the questions and answers in 2A.**

3 Real-life math

Work with your classmates. Use the running times in the movie ads in 1A to answer the questions.

1. Emily is going to see *Rain in My Eyes* at 9:30.

   Can she take the 11:15 bus home?

   _____.

2. Asha is going to take her children to see *My Friend, Green George* at 6:00.

   They live ten minutes from the movie theatre. Can they be home at 7:30?

   _____.

> **TEST YOURSELF** ✔
>
> Work with a partner. Use the movie ads in 1A to make plans this weekend.
> Partner A: Name a movie you want to see. Partner B: Ask about the times
> and ticket prices. Then change roles.

FOCUS ON
Socio-linguistic competence:
• Greeting card/e-card culture

1 Get ready to read

A Read the definitions.

occasion: a holiday, birthday, or other special day
greeting cards: cards for holidays, birthdays, and other special occasions

B Work with your classmates. Can you name the month for each holiday?

2 Read about greeting cards

A Read the article.

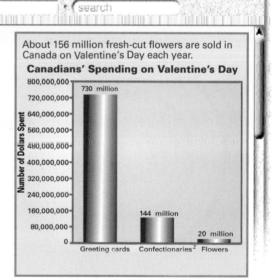

Greetings for All Occasions

GREETING CARDS FOR ALL OCCASIONS

Did you know...?
- People in Canada buy over 600 million cards every year.
- The number of cards produced in North America is approximately 2.5 billion!
- The number of cards produced every day in Canada is approximately 800,000.
- After Christmas, Valentine's Day is the second largest card-sending occasion.
- Mother's Day was first celebrated in 1914.
- Dads receive fifty percent of all Father's Day cards. Husbands receive twenty percent of all Father's Day cards, and the rest of the cards go to grandfathers.

About 156 million fresh-cut flowers are sold in Canada on Valentine's Day each year.

Canadians' Spending on Valentine's Day

Source: *The University of Western Ontario*
Source: *Hallmark Canada*

[1] billion =1,000,000,000
[2] confectionaries = dessert or candy

B Listen and read the article again.

☑ Describe different ways to look up information (CLB 3, 4 S)
144 ☑ Interpret information about greeting cards; use a phone book (CLB 3, 4 R)

C Complete the sentences. Use the words in the box.

holidays	birthday	~~Valentine's Day cards~~	Internet

1. North Americans buy forty million _Valentine's Day cards_ every year.
2. People buy greeting cards for birthdays and _____.
3. Some greeting cards are free on the _____.
4. A person usually gets a greeting card on his or her _____.

D Read the sentences. Write the answers.

1. Name three occasions when people buy greeting cards. _____
2. Name two places you can buy or get greeting cards. _____

3 Learn to use a phone book

A Look at the phone book. Answer the questions.

▶ **Holiday/Party Supply Stores**

BALLOONS AND THINGS·············· 555-2759
(see our display ad this page)

Hall's Card Shop ······················ 555-0225

Nancy's Cards and Gifts ··········· 555-7730

Paul's Flowers ························· 555-3151

SPECIAL MOMENTS GIFTS ········· 555-1351
(see our display ad this page)

HAPPY BIRTHDAY **BALLOONS** AND **THINGS**

All your party decorations here!

Open 9:00 a.m.–8:00 p.m.
7 days

Special Moments Gifts

Birthdays!
Anniversaries! Valentine's Day!
Something for everyone.

Open 9–9. Closed on Sundays

10% OFF THE PRICE WITH THIS AD

1. What's the phone number for Hall's Card Shop? _The phone number is 555-0225._
2. Where can you shop for flowers? _____
3. What time does Balloons and Things open every day? _____
4. Where can you get 10% off the price of gifts? _____
5. What store is closed on Sunday? _____

B Think about the questions. Talk about the answers with your class.

1. What information can you find in the phone book?
2. What are some other ways to find information about places in your city?

BRING IT TO LIFE

Look in the phone book. Is there a holiday or greeting card store near your home? Bring the address to class.

FOCUS ON

Problem solving:
• Determine how to modify plans

1 Grammar

A Circle *a* or *b*.

1. Was it cloudy yesterday?
   a. Yes, it was.
   b. No, it isn't.
2. Is it raining today?
   a. Yes, it was.
   b. No, it isn't.
3. Is it going to snow tomorrow?
   a. Yes, it was.
   b. No, it isn't.
4. Was it hot yesterday?
   a. Yes, it was.
   b. No, it isn't.

> **Grammar note**
>
> **Questions with *be***
>
> **Present**
> A: Is it sunny today?
> B: Yes, it is. *or*
>   No, it isn't.
>
> **Past**
> A: Was it sunny yesterday?
> B: Yes, it was. *or*
>   No, it wasn't.
>
> **Future**
> A: Is it going to be sunny tomorrow?
> B: Yes, it is. *or*
>   No, it isn't.

B Match the questions with the answers.

___d___ 1. Is it going to be sunny tomorrow?   a. He's going to work.

_____ 2. Is Joe going to study this evening?   b. Yes, he is.

_____ 3. What's he going to do tomorrow?   c. No, I'm not.

_____ 4. Are you going to cook next weekend?   d. Yes, it is.

C Unscramble the sentences.

1. next / be / going to / It's / cloudy / week ___It's going to be cloudy next week.___

2. this / going to / He's / at home / be / evening _____.

3. They're / going to / test / next / have / a / Friday _____.

4. tomorrow / are / What / going to / do / you _____?

D Complete the story. Use the words in the box.

going	it's	clean	be	~~is~~	sleep	Sunday	to

Max ___is___ listening to the weather report for the weekend. It's going to
       1
_____ sunny on Saturday. Max is _____ to have a picnic. It's going _____
      2   3   4
rain on Sunday morning. Max is going to stay in bed and _____. _____ going
                                                              5   6
to be cloudy on _____ afternoon. Max is going to _____ the house.
                     7   8

2 Group work

A Work with 2–3 classmates. Write 5 questions and answers about the pictures on page 137. Use *be going to.* Talk about the sentences with your class.

What are they going to do this summer?
They're going to go to the beach.

B Interview 3 classmates. Write their answers in your notebook.

ASK:

1. Are you going to see your friends this weekend?
2. Are you going to go to a party this weekend?
3. What are you going to do on Sunday?

Classmate #1 –Ben
1. Yes, he is.
2. No, he isn't.
3. He's going to go to the library.

C Talk about the answers with the class.

PROBLEM SOLVING

A Listen and read about Linda. What is her problem?

Linda lives in Winnipeg. Every year she drives two hours to her brother's house on Thanksgiving Day. Tomorrow is Thanksgiving. Linda is cooking and listening to the radio. The radio says that it's going to snow all night tonight and all day tomorrow. Linda doesn't like to drive in bad weather.

Snow...

B Work with your classmates. Answer the question. (More than one answer is possible.)

What should Linda do?
  a. Drive to her brother's house now.
  b. Stay home and watch TV.
  c. Take the bus to her brother's house.
  d. Other: _____

C Work with your classmates. What should Linda tell her brother? Write 3 sentences.

THE FIRST STEP: Names and Numbers

Pg. 2 Exercise 1C

M = Man, W = Woman
1. W: Maria. M-A-R-I-A.
2. M: Lee. L-E-E.
3. W: Tom. T-O-M.
4. M: Rebecca. R-E-B-E-C-C-A.
5. W: Kumar. K-U-M-A-R.
6. M: David. D-A-V-I-D.

Pg. 3 Exercise 3C

M = Man, W = Woman
1. W: Twenty
2. M: Forty
3. W: Ninety
4. M: One hundred

UNIT 1 In the Classroom

Pg. 4 Lesson 1—Exercise 1B

M = Man, W = Woman
1. W: Listen to the letter "A."
2. M: Point to the letter "B."
3. W: Say the letter "C."
4. M: Repeat the letter "D."
5. W: Open the notebook.
6. M: Close the book.
7. W: Sit down, please.
8. M: Stand up, please.

Pg. 5 Lesson 1—Exercise 2B

M = Man, W = Woman, N = Narrator
1. W: What is it?
   M: It's a board. This is a white board. There are numbers on the white board today.
   N: board
2. M: Who is he?
   W: He's a teacher, Mr. Terrel. He's a good teacher.
   N: teacher
3. M: What is it?
   W: It's a clock. The clock is on the wall. It is 10:00.
   N: clock
4. W: Who are they?
   M: They're students. There are two students.
   N: students
5. M: What is it?
   W: It's a dictionary. The dictionary is open.
   N: dictionary
6. W: What are they?
   M: They're notebooks. There are three red notebooks.
   N: notebooks
7. M: What are they?
   W: They're pens. There are five blue pens.
   N: pens

8. W: What is it?
   M: It's a desk. There are many things on the desk.
   N: desk
9. W: What are they?
   M: They're books. There are four books.
   N: books
10. M: What are they?
    W: They are chairs. The chairs are black. They're two black chairs.
    N: chairs

Pg. 6 Lesson 2—Exercise 1A

S = Woman school clerk, J = Jim Santos
S: Tell me your first name.
J: Jim.
S: Please spell your last name.
J: S-A-N-T-O-S.
S: Complete the form. Please print your address.
J: OK.
S: Write your telephone number with the area code. Then write your email address. Sign your name on line five. Please give me the form. Welcome to school.

Pg. 7 Lesson 2—Exercise 3A

W = Woman, M = Man
1. W: Circle the last name.
2. M: Circle the telephone number.
3. W: Circle the area code.
4. M: Circle the email address.
5. W: Circle the first name.
6. M: Circle the signature.

Pg. 7 Lesson 2—Exercise 3B

W = Woman, M = Man
1. W: Print your first name.
2. M: Write your telephone number.
3. W: Print your last name.
4. M: Write your address.
5. W: Sign your name.
6. M: Write your area code.

Pg. 11 Lesson 4—Exercise 2B

W = Woman, M = Man
1. W: What is your name?
2. M: I'm John.
3. M: Who's your teacher?
4. W: My teacher is Carol Brown.
5. M: What's your name?

UNIT 2 My Classmates

Pg. 16 Lesson 1—Exercise 1B

W = Woman, M = Man
1. W: What time is it?
   M: It's eight o'clock in the morning. Jun is at home.
2. M: What time is it?
   W: It's nine fifteen a.m. Jun's at work.
3. W: What time is it?
   M: It's noon. Time for lunch.

4. M: What time is it?
   W: It's eight thirty p.m. He's at school.
5. W: What time is it?
   M: It's nine forty-five. Jun's at home.
6. M: What time is it?
   W: It's midnight. Jun's at home.

Pg. 17 Lesson 1—Exercise 2B

W = Woman, M = Man, N = Narrator
1. W: The month is March.
   N: month
2. W: What is the first day of the workweek?
   M: Monday is the first day.
   N: day
3. W: The date for my first English class is March 8th, 2008.
   M: 3/8/08 is the date.
   N: date
4. M: One week is seven days. The week is from Sunday to Saturday.
   N: week
5. M: What day was yesterday?
   W: Yesterday was Monday, March 5th.
   N: yesterday
6. M: What day is today?
   W: Today is March 6th. It's a beautiful day today.
   N: today
7. W: Tomorrow is March 7th.
   M: I'll see you tomorrow.
   N: tomorrow
8. M: How many months are in a year?
   W: There are twelve months in a year.
   N: year

Pg. 19 Lesson 2—Exercise 3A

W1 = Woman 1, W2 = Woman 2, M1 = Man 1,
M2 = Man 2
1. W1: What's your name?
   M1: My name is James. That's J-A-M-E-S.
   W1: Where are you from?
   M1: I'm from China.
2. M1: What's your name?
   W1: My name is Lan. That's L-A-N.
   M1: Where are you from?
   W1: I'm from Vietnam.
3. M2: What's your name?
   W2: My name is Shoreh. That's S-H-O-R-E-H.
   M2: Where are you from?
   W2: I'm from Iran.
4. W2: What's your name?
   M2: My name is Pedro. That's P-E-D-R-O.
   W2: Where are you from?
   M2: I'm from the Philippines.

Pg. 19 Lesson 2—Exercise 3B

W = Woman, M = Man
1. W: What's your name?
2. M: Where are you from?
3. W: What's your date of birth?
4. M: What's your favourite colour?

Pg. 23 Lesson 4—Exercise 1E

M = Man, W = Woman, W2 = Woman 2, A = Announcer
1. M: What's your name?
   W: Pat Tyson. Mrs. Pat Tyson.
   M: Nice to meet you, Mrs. Tyson.
2. M: Good evening. I'm Pat Song. Welcome to class.
   W: Good evening, Mr. Song.
3. M: I have an appointment with Ms. Terry Miller.
   W: Yes. Ms. Miller can see you now.
4. W: Excuse me. My registration form says my teacher is Mrs. Terry Farmer.
   W2: I'm Mrs. Farmer. Welcome to class.
5. W: Hello. I'm Jean Silver.
   W2: Hello, Ms. Silver. Nice to meet you.
6. A: Attention! Paging Mr. Gold. Paging Mr. Gene Gold. Please come to the office. You have a phone call.

Pg. 23 Lesson 4—Exercise 2B

M = Man, W = Woman
W: OK, Mr. Milovich. I need to complete this form with you. Let's see, the date today is October 26th, 2008. Let me write that down…ten, twenty-six, oh-eight. What is your first name?
M: My first name is Sasha. That's S-A-S-H-A. Sasha.
W: OK. Are you married or single?
M: I'm single.
W: OK. Single. Let's see. What's your date of birth?
M: My date of birth is June 10th, 1971.
W: That's 6/10/71. Alright. Where are you from, Mr. Milovich?
M: I'm from Russia.
W: What's your address?
M: It's 3803 Elbow Dr. SW, Calgary, Alberta, T2S 2J9.
W: What's your phone number?
M: My phone number is area code four zero three, five five five, one six six nine.
W: Did you say four zero three, five five five, one six six nine?
M: Yes, that's right.

UNIT 3   Family and Friends

Pg. 28 Lesson 1—Exercise 1B

M = Man, W = Woman, W2 = Woman 2, A = Announcer
A: The Martinez family.
1. W: This picture is from June 22nd, 1997. Carlos and Anita are married. It's their wedding day.
   W2: Anita is Carlos' new wife. She is happy to be a wife.
2. M: Carlos is a new husband today. He is very happy to be a husband.
3. W: This picture is from Novembwer 15th, 1999. That's Carlos and Eric.
   M: Carlos is a father today. He's a little nervous about being a father.
4. W2: Eric is his new son. Eric's a beautiful boy
5. W: This picture is from April 20th, 2003.
   W2: Anita is a wonderful mother.

6. W: Her new daughter is Robin. She's a beautiful girl.
7. W2: This is a photograph of the Martinez family on June 30th, 2006.
    M: Carlos and Anita are busy parents. Soon they'll be very busy parents.
8. W: Eric and Robin are the only two children in this picture. Soon there will be three children.

Pg. 29 Lesson 1—Exercise 2B

E = Eric (age 10), N = Narrator
    E: Hi. I'm Eric and this is my family. They are all great people.
1. E: These are my grandparents. They are the best grandparents in the world.
    N: grandparents
2. E: This is my grandmother. Her name is Helen, but I call her Grandma. She's a really great grandmother.
    N: grandmother
3. E: My grandfather is Ramiro. We play together a lot. My grandfather is really funny.
    N: grandfather
4. E: My parents are Carlos and Anita, but they are Mom and Dad to me. I love my parents very much.
    N: parents
5. E: Hector is my uncle. Uncle Hector and my dad are brothers.
    N: uncle
6. E: That's my aunt. Her name is Sue. Aunt Sue makes the best chocolate cake.
    N: aunt
7. E: This is Robin. She is my sister. She's a good little sister—most of the time.
    N: sister
8. E: This is my new brother. He's one year old. My brother's name is Jimmy.
    N: brother
9. E: I have a cousin. Her name is Sandra. I visit my cousin every Sunday.
    N: cousin

Pg. 31 Lesson 2—Exercise 3A

M = Man, W = Woman
1. M: Simon is Paulina's husband. He is the man with grey hair and brown eyes.
2. W: Karina is Paulina's daughter. She is the girl with brown hair and blue eyes.
3. M: Sam is Paulina's son. He is the boy with blond hair and brown eyes.

Pg. 34 Lesson 4—Exercise 1A

W = Woman
W: Today is March 1st. March is my favourite month. There are a lot of special days in March. Look at my calendar. March 2nd is my friend Ashley's birthday. The first day of spring is March 20th. My friend Julie's birthday is on March 23rd.

Pg. 35 Lesson 4—Exercise 2A

M = Man, W = Woman
1. Digital answering machine voice: October 5th, 3:00 p.m.

M: Hi. It's me, Tim. Please call me at 555-9241. I'll be here all afternoon. Again, that's 5-5-5, 9-2-4-1.
2. Digital answering machine voice: February 21st, 9:45 a.m.
    W: Hello, Martha. It's Jackie calling. It's about 9:45 on February 21st. I just wanted to say, "Happy Birthday." Hope you are having a great day. Call me if you can. 555-7737. That's 5-5-5, 7-7-3-7.
3. Digital answering machine voice: May 18th, 7:30 p.m.
    M: This is Jim calling. My number is 5-5-5, 1-0-8-9. It's about 7:30 in the evening, Friday, May 18th. Are you there? Hello? Hello? Hello? OK. See you Monday.

Pg. 35 Lesson 4—Exercise 3B

M = Man, W = Woman
1. F: Teresa's birthday is January third.
2. M: My birthday is July twenty-sixth.
3. F: Armando's birthday is October seventh.
4. M: My mother's birthday is April fourteenth.
5. F: My birthday is September first.
6. M: My daughter's birthday is August twenty-third.

UNIT 4   At Home

Pg. 40 Lesson 1—Exercise 1B

M = Man, M2 = Man 2, W = Woman, W2 = Woman 2
1. W: Is the bathroom pink?
    W2: Yes, it is. The bathroom is a very pretty pink.
2. M: Is the bedroom brown?
    M2: No, it isn't. The bedroom is blue.
3. W: What colour is the garage?
    M: The garage is grey.
4. M: What colour is the living room?
    M2: The living room is green.
5. W: What colour is the dining area?
    W2: The dining area is yellow.
6. M: Is the kitchen green or white?
    W: The kitchen is white.

Pg. 41 Lesson 1—Exercise 2B

L = Lisa, K = Ken, N = Narrator
L: Hi, I'm Lisa. I live in an apartment on the second floor. I really like my apartment.
1. L: Here's the bedroom. This is my dresser. It's new.
    N: dresser
2. L: Look at my bookcase. I have many books in the bookcase.
    N: bookcase
3. L: Here's my bed. The bed is new, too.
    N: bed
4. L: Here's the bathroom. Look at the sink. The bathroom sink is new.
    N: sink
5. L: The bathtub is great. It's a big, old bathtub.
    N: bathtub
    K: Hello. My name is Ken. My apartment is on the first floor.
6. K: There's my living room. My couch looks good there. It's a comfortable couch.
    N: couch

7. K: Do you see that chair? It's my favourite chair for reading.
    N: chair
8. K: The living room rug is old. Maybe I'll get a new rug soon.
    N: rug
9. K: My TV is perfect there. I like to watch TV.
    N: TV
10. K: I spend a lot of time in the kitchen. That's my kitchen table. I eat and do homework at that table.
    N: table
11. K: I like the stove. It's a gas stove.
    N: stove
12. K: The refrigerator is nice, too. It's a big refrigerator.
    N: refrigerator

Pg. 43 Lesson 2—Exercise 3A

T = Tina, S = Sally

T: Sally, how about this TV? It's perfect for our house.
S: No, this TV is so small. Look at that TV! It's big. It's beautiful. It's perfect for our apartment.
T: Ummm…are you sure?
S: Tina, look at these chairs. They look comfortable and brown is a great colour.
T: No, these chairs are terrible! Look at those chairs. They're beautiful. Green is my favourite colour. They're perfect for our place.
S: Uhhhhh…are you sure?

Pg. 46 Lesson 4—Exercise 1B

M1 = Man 1, M2 = Man 2, M3 = Man 3, M4 = Man 4,
W1 = Woman 1, W2 = Woman 2, W3 = Woman 3,
W4 = Woman 4

1. M1: Please pay the gas bill today. It's seventeen dollars.
    W1: Seventeen dollars? That's not bad.
2. W2: What's the date?
    M2: It's September 29th.
    W2: Oh! Don't forget to pay the phone bill. It's twenty-six dollars.
    M2: Yes, dear. Twenty-six dollars. I'm paying it right now.
3. M3: When is the electric bill due?
    W3: It's due on October 1st. Please pay it. It's eighty-two dollars.
    M3: Eighty-two dollars? That's a lot of money.
4. M4: Is today the 14th?
    W4: Yes, it is. We need to pay the water bill. It's fourteen dollars and fifty cents and it's due tomorrow.
    M4: Fourteen fifty? OK, I can pay it tomorrow morning.

UNIT 5 In the Neighbourhood

Pg. 52 Lesson 1—Exercise 1B

M1 = Man 1, M2 = Man 2, W1 = Woman 1,
W2 = Woman 2

1. W1: Excuse me, where's the school?
    M1: The high school is on 2nd Street.

2. M1: Is there a grocery store on 2nd Street?
    W1: Yes, there's a grocery store on 2nd Street.
3. M1: Excuse me, where's the hospital? I think I'm lost.
    M2: The hospital is on Elm Street between 2nd and 3rd.
4. W1: Is there a bank nearby?
    W2: Yes. The bank is on Oak Street on the corner of 1st and Oak.
5. M1: Can you tell me where the fire station is?
    W1: No problem. The fire station is on 1st Street.
6. M1: Can I help you?
    W1: Yes, please. Where is the police station?
    M1: The police station is on Pine Street.

Pg. 53 Lesson 1—Exercise 2B

M = Man, N = Narrator

    M: Hello. My name is Mark. I live in Riverside. This is my neighbourhood.
1. M: I go to the supermarket every Monday. Fast Mart is a good supermarket.
    N: supermarket
2. M: The pharmacy is on the corner. When I need medicine, I go to the pharmacy.
    N: pharmacy
3. M: I go to the movies every Friday. Tonight I'm going to see *Hometown Friends* at the movie theatre.
    N: movie theatre
4. M: The car on the street is blue. That's my friend Sam driving the car.
    N: car
5. M: There's a stop sign on the corner. Don't forget to stop at the stop sign!
    N: stop sign
6. M: Here comes the school bus. The children are riding the bus to school.
    N: bus
7. M: A girl is waiting at the bus stop. She goes to the bus stop every morning at 7:45.
    N: bus stop
8. M: Bob's Restaurant is my favourite restaurant in town!
    N: restaurant
9. M: The gas station is near the park. I work at that gas station.
    N: gas station
10. M: The parking lot is over there. There is one parking lot on this street.
    N: parking lot
11. M: Town Savings is my bank. It's a good bank.
    N: bank
12. M: There's a boy riding a bicycle. Do you like to ride a bicycle?
    N: bicycle

Pg. 55 Lesson 2—Exercise 3A

M1 = Man 1, M2 = Man 2, M3 = Man 3, M4 = Man 4,
M5 = Man 5, W1= Woman 1, W2 = Woman 2,
W3 = Woman 3, W4 = Woman 4, W5 = Woman 5

1. W1: Excuse me, where's the parking lot?
    M1: It's behind the pharmacy.

2. M2: (Sneezing) Excuse me. Where is the clinic?
   W2: The clinic is between the parking lot and the apartment building.
3. W3: Where's the supermarket?
   M3: It's in front of the apartment building.
4. M4: Excuse me. Is there a hospital on Lee Street?
   W4: Yes, it's across from the pharmacy.
5. W5: Is there a fire station on this street?
   M5: Yes. The fire station is next to the post office.

Pg. 58 Lesson 4—Exercise 1B

W = Woman
W: 1. Let me give you directions to the clinic from here. Go straight on Grand Avenue.
   2. Turn right on 12th Street.
   3. Go two blocks on Maple Street.
   4. Turn left on 14th Street.
   5. It's across from the park.
   6. It's next to the pharmacy.

UNIT 6 Daily Routines

Pg. 64 Lesson 1—Exercise 1B

M = Man, W = Woman
M: Good morning! My name's Brian.
W: And I'm Jen.
M: This is our daily routine.
1. M: In the morning, we get up at 7 a.m.
   W: Yes. We get up at 7:00.
2. W: We get dressed at 7:15.
   M: Uh-huh. 7:15 is when we get dressed.
3. M: At 7:30 we eat breakfast.
   W: That's right. Before we go to work, we eat breakfast.
4. W: In the evening, we come home at 5:30.
   M: It's nice to come home together.
5. W: We make dinner at 6:00.
   M: Yes, we make dinner together.
6. W: We usually go to bed at 11:00 p.m. Right, honey?
   M: Yes, that's right. We go to bed at 11:00.
   M and W: That's it. That's our daily routine!

Pg. 65 Lesson 1—Exercise 2B

W = Woman, N = Narrator
1. W: On school days, Deka and her friend walk to school together. They practise English while they walk.
   N: walk to school
2. W: After class, Deka and her friends have lunch. They usually have lunch in the cafeteria.
   N: have lunch
3. W: Deka has to ride the bus for 15 minutes. She likes to ride the bus to her job.
   N: ride the bus
4. W: Deka works at a supermarket. She has to work there Monday through Friday.
   N: work
5. W: In the evening, Deka has to do housework. She likes to do housework.
   N: do housework

6. W: When the house is clean, she takes a shower. She likes to take a hot shower and relax.
   N: take a shower
7. W: Deka drinks coffee to stay awake. She likes to drink coffee.
   N: drink coffee
8. W: Deka thinks that doing homework is very important. At the end of the day, Deka has time to do homework.
   N: do homework
9. W: Deka is tired after a long day. At midnight, it's time for her to go to bed.
   N: go to bed

Pg. 67 Lesson 2—Exercise 3A

MB = Mel Brown
Mel: I'm Mel. I work at Joe's Market and I like my job a lot. Joe's is a small market in my neighbourhood. I work on Monday, Wednesday, and Friday from 10:00 in the morning to 3:00 in the afternoon. In the morning, I mop the floor and wash the windows. In the afternoon, I help the manager and answer the phone. The hours are good and the people are nice. It's a great job for me.

Pg. 71 Lesson 4—Exercise 1E

M = Man, W = Woman, W1 = Woman 1, W2 = Woman 2
1. M: Excuse me. The photocopier is out of paper. Can you help me?
   W: Sure. You need to fill the machine. Put the paper here.
   M: Oh, that's easy. Thanks for your help.
2. W: I think the printer is broken. It doesn't print.
   M: No, it's OK. Just turn on the printer. Push this button.
   W: Oops! My mistake. I'll turn it on.
3. M: Excuse me. The stapler is empty. Do you have another one?
   W: No, let's fill the stapler. Put the staples here.
   M: OK. Thanks.
4. W1: Excuse me, Mrs. Blake. Can you help me? How do you turn off the computer?
   W2: Push this button.
   W1: Oh! OK, thank you.

UNIT 7 Shop and Spend

Pg. 76 Lesson 1, Exercise 1B

M1 = Man 1, M2 = Man 2, W1 = Woman 1,
W2 = Woman 2, B1 = Boy 1, B2 = Boy 2
1. W1: Can I have a penny? I need to buy a one-cent stamp.
   M1: Sure. Here's a penny.
2. B1: Can I have a nickel? I want some gum.
   W2: Yes, honey. Here's a nickel.
3. B1: Candy is 10 cents. I need a dime.
   B2: Here's a dime.
4. W1: I need to buy a pencil. It costs a quarter.
   W2: A pencil is a quarter? I'll buy one, too.
5. M1: How much is coffee? I only have a loonie.
   W1: That's OK. Coffee is one dollar.

6. M2: I have a five-dollar bill. Is that enough for the book?
   W2: Yes, the book is five dollars.
7. W1: The gas bill is forty-five dollars this month. Please write a cheque.
   M1: I have the cheque right here.
8. M1: We need a money order for the rent.
   W2: I have a money order for $300 right here.

Pg. 77 Lesson 1—Exercise 2B

W = Woman, N = Narrator
1. W: There are many customers in the store. One customer is waiting in line.
   N: customer
2. W: The cashier takes money and gives change. It's important to give correct change.
   N: change
3. W: The lady in line is buying a dress. It's a blue dress.
   N: dress
4. W: She is also buying some shoes. The shoes are on the counter.
   N: shoes
5. W: There are some socks next to the shoes. The socks are on sale.
   N: socks
6. W: That man with the bag is wearing a suit. It's a brown suit.
   N: suit
7. W: Men's shirts are on sale. For only $19.99, you can buy this shirt.
   N: shirt
8. W: Ties are on sale, too. Do you need a tie?
   N: tie
9. W: The salesperson is wearing a blouse. Her blouse is yellow.
   N: blouse
10. W: The salesperson is also wearing a skirt. She usually wears a skirt to work.
    N: skirt
11. W: The salesperson is helping a young man in a T-shirt. He's wearing a red T-shirt.
    N: T-shirt
12. W: The young man is also wearing grey pants. He might buy some new pants today.
    N: pants

Pg. 79 Lesson 2—Exercise 3A

J = John
J: My name is John. These are the clothes I like to wear. At home, I usually wear a T-shirt and jeans. I also wear my favourite runners. At work, I wear a hat, a uniform, and a belt. On special occasions, I like to look good. I wear my favourite suit, tie, and shoes. How about you? What clothes do you like to wear?

Pg. 83 Lesson 4—Exercise 1E

M = Man Customer, S = Salesperson, W = Woman Customer
1. M: Excuse me. Is this jacket a large? I need a large.
   S: Yes, it is. It's eighty dollars.
   M: Did you say eighteen or eighty?
   S: It's eighty dollars.
   M: OK, thanks. I'll think about it.
2. S: Can I help you with something?
   W: Yes. This blouse and this skirt are beautiful. What size are they?
   S: They're both small.
   W: Are they on sale?
   S: Yes, they are. The blouse is seventeen dollars and the skirt is only sixteen dollars.
   W: Great! I'll take them both in small.
3. M: Excuse me. I need a medium jacket and a medium T-shirt.
   S: These are medium.
   M: How much are they?
   S: The jacket is nineteen ninety-nine and the T-shirts are on sale for five dollars each.

Pg. 83 Lesson 4—Exercise 2C

M = Man, W = Woman
1. M: How much are the shoes?
   W: They're fifty dollars.
2. W: How much is the shirt?
   M: It's sixteen dollars.
3. W: That's one dress and one sweater. Your total is forty twenty-eight.
4. M: OK. Here you go. Your change is twelve sixty.
5. W: That tie is on sale. It's ten eighteen.
6. M: Thank you very much. Your change is six dollars and ninety cents.

UNIT 8   Eating Well

Pg. 88 Lesson 1—Exercise 1B

M1 = Man 1, M2 = Man 2, W1 = Woman 1, W2 = Woman 2
1. W1: I need to buy fruit.
   M1: Fruit? We have a special on bananas.
2. M1: What vegetables are fresh today?
   W1: Vegetables? We have fresh lettuce and carrots.
3. M1: The man in the white shirt is carrying a basket.
   W1: The basket is blue.
4. M1: The red shopping cart is outside.
   W1: A woman is pushing the cart.
5. M1: What is the cashier doing?
   M2: The cashier is ringing up the food.
6. W1: The young man is the bagger.
   W2: The bagger is putting the food in bags.

Pg. 89 Lesson 1—Exercise 2B

W = Woman, N = Narrator
1. W: I go to the supermarket every week. This week, I'm buying bananas. Everyone in my family eats bananas.
   N: bananas

2. W: These apples look delicious. I always put apples in the kids' lunches.
   N: apples
3. W: Lettuce is on sale this week. I can make a salad with lettuce for dinner.
   N: lettuce
4. W: Milk is expensive this week, but my kids drink milk every day.
   N: milk
5. W: I'm buying a dozen eggs. There's a sale on eggs this week.
   N: eggs
6. W: Look at these beautiful red tomatoes. My husband loves tomatoes.
   N: tomatoes
7. W: I buy bread every week. My kids like white bread.
   N: bread
8. W: This is my favourite soup. I like to have soup for lunch.
   N: soup
9. W: I'm making chicken for dinner tonight. My whole family likes chicken.
   N: chicken
10. W: These are nice sweet onions. My son loves onions.
    N: onions
11. W: I buy grapes when they are on sale. Grapes are a healthy snack.
    N: grapes
12. W: I'm also buying potatoes. Tomorrow, we'll have potatoes with dinner.
    N: potatoes

Pg. 91 Lesson 2—Exercise 3B

M = Mr. Garcia, MS = Mrs. Garcia
MS: OK, let's see what's on sale this week. Ground beef is $6.79 per kilogram. That's great. We need ground beef. Peanut butter is $3.99. No, that's too expensive. We need tuna fish and carrots. We don't need beans and we don't need spaghetti this week. Oh, that's my favourite cheese! It's $5.67 per kilogram. It's on sale this week. I can have a little cheese. Ramon? Do you need anything special from the supermarket?
M: Well, don't forget my oranges.
MS: OK, oranges.

Pg. 95 Lesson 4—Exercise 1E

P1 = Pizza Store Employee 1, P2 = Pizza Store Employee 2, P3 = Pizza Store Employee 3, C1 = Woman Customer 1, C2 = Man Customer, C3 = Woman Customer 2
1. P1: Are you ready to order?
   C1: Yes, I am. I'd like two large pizzas with onions and one small pizza with pepperoni.
   P1: Anything to drink?
   C1: Yes, please. I'd like one small pop.
   P1: That's two large pizzas with onions, one small pizza with pepperoni, and one small pop.
   C1: Yes, that's right.

2. P2: Are you ready to order?
   C2: Yes, I'm ready. I'd like one medium pizza with peppers.
   P2: That's one medium pizza with peppers. Anything to drink?
   C2: Yes. Two large iced teas and one medium pop.
   P2: One medium pizza with peppers, two large iced teas, and one medium pop coming up.
3. P3: Are you ready to order?
   C3: Yes, I'm ready. I'd like two small pizzas with onions and mushrooms.
   P3: OK, anything to drink?
   C3: Yes, please. I'd like one small pop and two large iced teas.
   P3: That's two small pizzas with onions and mushrooms, one small pop, and two large iced teas.
   C3: That's right. Thank you.

Pg. 95 Lesson 4—Exercise 2B

M = Man, W = Woman
1. M: I'd like a large pizza.
2. W: Do you want anything to drink?
3. M: Are you ready to order?
4. W: I never eat lunch at home.

UNIT 9 Your Health

Pg. 100 Lesson 1—Exercise 1B

R = Receptionist, W1 = Woman 1, W2 = Woman 2, W3 = Woman 3, M1 = Man 1, M2 = Man 2, M3 = Man 3
1. R: Doctor's office. How can I help you today?
   W1: This is Ming Lee calling. My head hurts.
2. R: Doctor's office. How can I help you today?
   M1: Hello. This is Miguel Diaz. I hurt my nose.
   R: I'm sorry to hear that.
   M1: Yes. I got hit in the nose with a baseball. It really hurts!
3. R: Hello, Ms. Singh. I understand that you need to see the doctor.
   W2: Yes. My neck hurts.
4. R: Is there anything else?
   W2: Yes. My back hurts, too.
5. R: Doctor's office. Can I help you?
   M2: This is Raji Patel. My chest hurts.
   R: Mr. Patel, do you need an ambulance?
   M2: No, it's not that bad. I just want to see the doctor.
6. R: Doctor's office? Can I help you?
   M3: Yes. This is Niles Gold. I have to see the doctor about my arm. My arm hurts.
7. R: Does anything else hurt?
   M3: Yes, my hand hurts, too.
8. R: So, Ms. Vega, do you need to see the doctor this week?
   W3: Yes I do. My foot hurts.
9. R: OK, Ms. Vega. The doctor can see you tomorrow at 11 a.m. Is there anything else?
   W3: Yes, my leg hurts, too.

Pg. 101 Lesson 1—Exercise 2B

M = Man, N = Narrator, N1 = Nurse
1. M: Hi. My name is Michael. I'm at the doctor's office. It's very busy at the doctor's office today.
   N: doctor's office
2. M: I'm sick. I have a stomach ache. It's no fun having a stomach ache.
   N: stomach ache
3. M: The lady next to me has an earache. She says she gets bad earaches twice a month.
   N: earache
4. M: I think the girl over there has a fever. Her face is hot and red. It's probably a fever.
   N: fever
5. M: The woman at the receptionist's window has a cold. I hope I don't get her cold!
   N: cold
6. M: The receptionist is talking to the woman with a cold. The receptionist is working hard today.
   N: receptionist
7. M: In fact, I think she has a headache. She has her hand on her head. Yes, I'm sure she has a headache.
   N: headache
8. M: The lady next to me, the girl over there, and I are all patients today. There are other patients here, too.
   N: patients
9. M: The man in the center of the room has a backache. It's terrible to have a backache.
   N: backache
10. M: Wow! That soccer player has a broken leg. I know from experience. It's no fun to have a broken leg.
    N: broken leg
11. M: The doctor is giving the man a prescription for some medicine. That's Doctor Kim. She's a great doctor.
    N: doctor
12. M: There's the nurse. She has a chart. I think she's looking for me.
    N1: Michael? Michael Chen?
    M: Excuse me, the nurse is calling me.
    N: nurse

Pg. 103 Lesson 2—Exercise 3B

D = Doctor, M1 = Man 1, M2 = Man 2, M3 = Man 3,
M4 = Man 4, W1 = Woman 1, W2 = Woman 2
1. D: What's the matter today Mr. Jones?
   M1: Well, Dr. Moss, I don't feel well. I have a stomach ache.
   D: When did it start?
   M1: Yesterday.
   D: Tell me about your diet, Mr. Jones.
   M1: I don't eat lunch. I drink a lot of pop and coffee.
   D: Mr. Jones, you have to change your diet.
2. D: How are you today, Mrs. Lynn?
   W1: Not so good. I have a terrible headache.
   D: Take this medicine.
   W1: Thanks, Doctor.

3. D: What seems to be the problem, Mr. Martinez?
   M2: Oh, Doctor Moss, I have a bad cold.
   D: Say "Ahhhh."
   M2: "Ahhhhhhhhhhhhhhhhhhhhhhhh."
   D: Yes, you have a cold. Drink a lot of fluids. Try hot tea or juice.
   M2: OK, Dr. Moss. Achoo!
   D: Bless you.
4. W2: I don't feel well. I sit at my desk and I'm tired all day, Dr. Moss.
   D: Ms. Mendoza, you have to exercise three or four times a week.
5. M3: I have a terrible backache today, Dr. Moss.
   D: You have to stay home and rest for forty-eight hours, Mr. White.
6. D: I'm worried about your blood pressure, Mr. Wang. You have to quit smoking.
   M4: Yes, Dr. Moss. I know.

Pg. 107 Lesson 4—Exercise 1E

MR = Man Receptionist, WR = Woman Receptionist,
M1 = Man 1, M2 = Man 2
1. MR: Good morning. Dr. Wu's Dental Clinic.
   M1: This is Tom Garcia. I have to make an appointment with the dentist.
   MR: OK. The first opening I have is on Tuesday, June 2nd at 4:00 in the afternoon. Is that OK?
   M1: 4:00 on Tuesday? Yes, that's fine.
   MR: OK, Tom. We'll see you at 4:00 on Tuesday, June 2nd.
2. WR: Dr. Brown's office. Can I help you?
   M2: Yes, this is Pat McGee. I have to see Dr. Brown for an eye examination.
   WR: OK, Pat. I have an appointment available on October 23rd at 10:30 a.m. Is that OK?
   M2: October 23rd? Yes, that's a Monday. That's fine.
   WR: OK, then. Thanks, Pat. See you on Monday, October 23rd at 10:30.

Pg. 107 Lesson 4—Exercise 3C

M = Man, W = Woman
1. W: What does he have to do today?
2. M: She has to work at 9:00.
3. W: Who has a new car?
4. M: We have two children.

UNIT 10 Getting the Job

Pg. 112 Lesson 1—Exercise 1B

M1 = Man 1, M2 = Man 2, M3 = Man 3, W1 = Woman 1,
W2 = Woman 2, W3 = Woman 3
1. M1: I work at the pharmacy. I fill prescriptions. I like my job because I help people feel better. I'm a pharmacist.
2. W1: I work in my home. I take care of my family and our home. It's a lot of work, but I love my family. I'm a homemaker.
3. M2: I work in a garage. I fix a lot of cars. My friends love my job because I fix their cars, too. I'm a mechanic.

4. M3: I work at a school. I keep the school buildings clean. I'm a janitor.
5. W2: I work at Fran's Fancy Restaurant. I am a server. I am the best server in the restaurant.
6. W3: I work at a day care centre. I take care of children all day. I love my job. I'm a childcare worker.

Pg. 113 Lesson 1—Exercise 2B

M1 = Man 1, N = Narrator, M2 = Man 2, M3 = Man 3, M4 = Man 4, M5 = Man 5, M6 = Man 6, W1 = Woman 1, W2 = Woman 2

1. M1: Hi. I'm Lars. I'm delivering food to the restaurant. I'm a delivery person.
   N: delivery person
2. W1: I'm Young Hee. Today is a very big day for me. I manage the restaurant. I'm the manager.
   N: manager
3. W2: I'm Nancy. Today is my first day. I serve food to the customers. I'm a server.
   N: server
4. M2: Hi. I'm Henry. I clean the tables and help Nancy. I'm the bus person.
   N: bus person
5. M3: Hello. I'm Tomas. I can't talk now. I'm busy. I have to cook the food. I'm the cook.
   N: cook
6. M4: I'm Pat. I'm fixing the sink now. I'm the plumber.
   N: plumber
7. M5: I'm Oliver. I'm painting the building for the big grand opening. I'm the painter.
   N: painter
8. M6: I'm Nate. I plant flowers. These are going to be beautiful. I'm a gardener.
   N: gardener

Pg. 119 Lesson 4—Exercise 1E

M1 = Man 1, M2 = Man 2, W1 = Woman 1, W2 = Woman 2, W3 = Woman 3

1. W1: My name is Gladys. I lived in El Salvador for twenty years. I was a full-time nurse. I can help patients.
2. M1: My name is Ken. I lived in Japan and studied English. I was a pharmacist. I can fill prescriptions.
3. M2: My name is Franco. I was a plumber in Mexico for many years. I can fix sinks and toilets.
4. W3: My name is Molly. I studied business and stayed home with my children for five years. I can cook, clean, pay bills, and take care of children.

Pg. 119 Lesson 4—Exercise 3B

M = Man, W = Woman
1. W: I can't fix the sink.
2. M: I can plant flowers.
3. W: I can take care of children.
4. M: I can't fill prescriptions.
5. W: I can't speak Spanish.
6. M: I can cook Mexican food.

UNIT 11 Safety First

Pg. 124 Lesson 1—Exercise 1B

M = Man, W = Woman
1. M: Be careful. There's a stop sign. You have to stop and look for other cars at a stop sign.
2. W: Be careful. That's a road work sign. You have to watch for people working on the street when you see a road work sign.
3. W: Look out! There's a school crossing sign. You have to slow down and look for children at a school crossing sign.
4. M: Don't park there. There's a "no parking" sign. You can't park next to a "no parking" sign. You have to park somewhere else.
5. W: The sign says "no left turn." You can't turn left. You can only turn right.
6. M: Slow down! The speed limit sign says "50." You have to pay attention to the speed limit sign.

Pg. 125 Lesson 1—Exercise 2B

W = Woman, N = Narrator
1. W: There's an emergency exit on the left. The emergency exit is always open during the workday.
   N: emergency exit
2. W: Ann and Joe are factory workers. These factory workers come to work at 7:30 a.m.
   N: factory workers
3. W: Joe is wearing his hard hat. He knows that a hard hat will keep his head safe.
   N: hard hat
4. W: Joe is also wearing safety glasses. He always wears his safety glasses at work.
   N: safety glasses
5. W: Joe is also wearing his safety gloves. Sometimes he works with chemicals. He always wears safety gloves then.
   N: safety gloves
6. W: Joe is wearing his safety boots, too. He wears his safety boots every day.
   N: safety boots
7. W: This warehouse is a safe workplace. A safe workplace is important for everybody.
   N: safe
8. W: There's a fire extinguisher on the wall. All the workers learn to use the fire extinguisher.
   N: fire extinguisher
9. W: Tanya is very careful at work. She pays attention and wears her safety equipment. She's a careful worker.
   N: careful
10. W: This warehouse is dangerous, or unsafe. It's important to pay attention to dangerous situations and things.
    N: dangerous, unsafe
11. W: Tim is careless at work. He never pays attention and he doesn't wear safety equipment. He's a careless worker.
    N: careless

12. W: Look out, Tim! The floor is wet! Tim doesn't see the wet floor.
    N: wet floor

Page 127 Lesson 2—Exercise 3A

NA = News Anchor
NA: Good evening. This is Leticia Gomez at Channel 13 News with tonight's special edition: Are you safe on the road, at work, and at home? Take the following quiz to find out.
1. Do you always drive the speed limit?
2. Do you drive fast near school crossings?
3. Do you know where the emergency exits are in the building?
4. Do you wear safety equipment at work?
5. Do you have a smoke detector in the kitchen? Remember to be safe. This is Leticia Gomez reporting. Good night.

Pg. 131 Lesson 4—Exercise 1E

M1 = Man 1, M2 = Man 2, M3 = Man 3, W1 = Woman 1, W2 = Woman 2, W3 = Woman 3
1. M1: 911. What's the emergency?
   W1: A car accident on my street.
   M1: Where is the accident?
   W1: On the corner of Pine Avenue and Hope Street.
   M1: Is anyone hurt?
   W1: Yes, a man.
   M1: OK. Help is on the way.
2. W2: 911. What's the emergency?
   M2: There's a robbery.
   W2: What's the address?
   M2: 3310 Main Street.
   W2: Is anyone hurt?
   M2: Yes, the manager.
   W2: OK, sir. A police officer is on the way.
3. W2: 911. What's your emergency?
   W3: There's a fire in the house across the street.
   W2: What's the address?
   W3: It's 615 Elm Street.
   W2: Is anyone hurt?
   W3: Yes, a young woman.
   W2: OK, I'll send an ambulance.
4. W2: 911. What's your emergency?
   M3: There's been a bad car accident.
   W2: Where's the accident?
   M3: It's on 1st Street.
   W2: Is anyone hurt?
   M3: Yes. Two men are hurt.

Pg. 131 Lesson 4—Exercise 2A

M = Mother, B = Boy, D = Daughter, F = Father
M: You should eat your vegetables.
B: Why? Why should I eat vegetables?
M: You should eat vegetables because they're good for you.
M: You shouldn't smoke.
D: I know I shouldn't. I shouldn't smoke because it's bad for me. Don't worry, Mom. I know.
M: You should wash the car.
F: I know I should. The car is dirty. I should wash it today.
M: You're right. You should wash it and I should help you.

Pg. 131 Lesson 4—Exercise 2B

M = Man, W = Woman
1. W: You shouldn't park there.
2. M: For a healthy diet, you should eat these.
3. W: At work, you should do this.
4. M: When you have a cold, you shouldn't do this.
5. M: When you are driving, you should do this.
6. W: At home, you shouldn't do this.

UNIT 12 Free Time

Pg. 136 Lesson 1—Exercise 1B

WM = Weatherman
1. WM: Hello and Happy New Year! It's snowing this New Year's. It's going to keep snowing all day.
2. WM: It's a little cloudy this Mother's Day. It's cloudy, but there's no rain. Go ahead and take Mom to the park for some fun.
3. WM: Hello, and Happy Father's Day. It's a beautiful sunny day today, so go out and enjoy the sunny weather with Dad.
4. WM: It's hot this Canada Day. It's hot at the park. It's hot at the beach. Wherever you go, drink lots of water and have a great July 1st.
5. WM: Yes, it's raining this Labour Day, so don't forget your umbrella. It's raining hard.
6. WM: Happy Thanksgiving, everyone. Brrrr! It sure is cold out. I'm going to get out of the cold and have some turkey with my family. Enjoy your holiday, everybody.

Pg. 137 Lesson 1—Exercise 2B

W = Woman, N = Narrator
1. W: In the winter, the weather is very cold in our city. We like to stay home. On snowy days, we stay home and relax together.
   N: stay home
2. W: When we have enough snow, the kids make a snowman. My son is outside making a snowman now.
   N: make a snowman
3. W: In the spring, the weather is usually nice. We like to go to the park and have a picnic. My daughter and I are getting ready to have a picnic now.
   N: have a picnic
4. W: My husband and my son love to play soccer. They are playing soccer now.
   N: play soccer
5. W: It's hot in our city in the summer. We like to go to the beach. In the summer, we go to the beach every weekend.
   N: go to the beach
6. W: There's a boy swimming in the ocean. On a hot summer day, it's great to go swimming.
   N: go swimming
7. W: The weather changes a lot in the fall here. Sometimes it's sunny. Sometimes it's cloudy and windy. When it's nice, we like to go out to eat. We go out to eat once or twice a month.
   N: go out to eat

8. W: We also like to go to the movies in the fall. Look.
        Some people across the street are going to go to
        the movies.
    N: go to the movies

Pg. 139 Lesson 2—Exercise 3A

M = Man, W = Woman
1. W: I'm taking the number one bus. What's the first
        stop?
    M: The number one bus stops at Grant Street at 8:00
        a.m.
2. M: What time does the number two bus stop at the
        school?
    W: It stops at Front Street School at 12:15.
3. W: I work at the mall. I have to be there at 9:00.
    M: You can take the number one bus. It stops at the
        mall at 8:30.
4. W: I'm taking my children to the hockey game. It
        starts at 5:00. What time does the number three
        bus stop at the hockey arena?
    M: The number three bus stops at the hockey arena
        at 4:45.
    W: Great!
5. W: Let's go to the park today for lunch. What time
        does the number two bus stop there?
    M: The number two stops at the park at 1:00. That's
        a good time for lunch!

Pg. 142 Lesson 4—Exercise 1E

N = Norma, G = Gloria
G: Hi, Norma.
N: Hi, Gloria. What are you doing?
G: I'm going to see a movie. Do you want to go with
    me?
N: Sure. What are you going to see?
G: I want to see *Rain in My Eyes*. It's a love story. It's
    playing at 9:30.
N: *Rain in My Eyes*? That sounds good. Let's go then.
G: OK. If we go at 9:30, and it's over by 11:30 we can
    take the last bus.
N: That's great! I'll meet you at the bus stop at 9:00.
G: OK. Bye.

Pg. 143 Lesson 4—Exercise 2B

M = Man, W = Woman
1. M: I'm going to go to the supermarket.
2. W: I wanna eat dinner at 6:00.
3. M: I want to study at the library tomorrow.
4. W: I'm gonna call my mother this evening.
5. M: Do you wanna go to the beach with us
        tomorrow?

GRAMMAR CHARTS

THE SIMPLE PRESENT WITH *BE*

Statements

I	am	
You	are	a student.
He / She	is	
It	is	a book.
We / You / They	are	students.

Negative statements

I	am not	
You	are not	a student.
He / She	is not	
It	is not	a book.
We / You / They	are not	students.

Contractions

I am = I'm	I am not = I'm not
you are = you're	you are not = you're not / you aren't
he is = he's	he is not = he's not / he isn't
she is = she's	she is not = she's not / she isn't
it is = it's	it is not = it's not / it isn't
we are = we're	we are not = we're not / we aren't
they are = they're	they are not = they're not / they aren't

Yes/No questions

Am	I	
Are	you	
Is	he / she / it	happy?
Are	we / you / they	

Answers

Yes,	I	am.
	you	are.
	he / she / it	is.
	we / you / they	are.

No,	I	am not.
	you	aren't.
	he / she / it	isn't.
	we / you / they	aren't.

Information questions

Where	am	I?
How	are	you?
Who	is	he? / she?
When	is	it?
Where / What	are	we? / you? / they?

THE PRESENT CONTINUOUS

Statements

I	am	
You	are	
He / She / It	is	sleeping.
We / You / They	are	

Negative statements

I	am not	
You	aren't	
He / She / It	isn't	sleeping.
We / You / They	aren't	

Yes/No questions

Am	I	
Are	you	
Is	he / she / it	eating?
Are	we / you / they	

Answers

Yes,	I	am.
	you	are.
	he / she / it	is.
	we / you / they	are.

No,	I	am not.
	you	aren't.
	he / she / it	isn't.
	we / you / they	aren't.

Information questions

Where	am	I	going?
When	are	you	
Who / Why	is	he / she	calling?
How	is	it	working?
What	are	we / you / they	doing?

THE SIMPLE PRESENT

Statements

I You	work.
He She It	works.
We You They	work.

Negative statements

I You	don't	
He She It	doesn't	work.
We You They	don't	

Contractions

do not = don't
does not = doesn't

Yes/No questions

Do	I you	
Does	he she it	work?
Do	we you they	

Answers

Yes,	I you	do.	No,	I you	don't.
	he she it	does.		he she it	doesn't.
	we you they	do.		we you they	don't.

Information questions

What	do	I you	study?
Who	does	he she	see?
How	does	it	work?
Where When Why	do	we you they	work?

THE SIMPLE PAST WITH *BE*

Statements

I	was	
You	were	
He She It	was	here.
We You They	were	

Negative statements

I	wasn't	
You	weren't	
He She It	wasn't	here.
We You They	weren't	

Contractions

was not = wasn't
were not = weren't

Yes/No questions

Was	I	
Were	you	
Was	he she it	late?
Were	we you they	

Answers

Yes,	I	was.	No,	I	wasn't.
	you	were.		you	weren't.
	he she it	was.		he she it	wasn't.
	we you they	were.		we you they	weren't.

Information questions

Where	was	I	yesterday?
Why	were	you	in Windsor?
Who	was	he? she?	
What	was	it?	
When	were	we	here?
How	were	you they	yesterday?

THE FUTURE WITH *BE GOING TO*

Statements

I	am		
You	are	going to	have a party tomorrow.
He She	is		
It	is	going to	rain in two days.
We You They	are	going to	visit friends next week.

Negative statements

I	am not		
You	aren't	going to	have a party tomorrow.
He She	isn't		
It	isn't	going to	rain in two days.
We You They	aren't	going to	visit friends next week.

Yes/No questions

Am	I		
Are	you	going to	work?
Is	he she		
Is	it	going to	snow?
Are	we you they	going to	go?

Answers

	I	am.		I	am not.	
	you	are.		you	aren't.	
Yes,	he she it	is.	No,	he she it	isn't.	
	we you they	are.		we you they	aren't.	

Information questions

Who	am	I	going to	see?
	are	you		
When What	is	he she it	going to	eat?
How Why What	are	we you they	going to	study?

CAN AND *SHOULD*

Statements

I You He She It We You They	can should	work.

Negative statements

I You He She It We You They	can't shouldn't	work.

Contractions

cannot = can't
should not = shouldn't

Yes/No questions

Can Should	I you he she it we you they	work?

Answers

Yes,	I you he she it we you they	can. should.	No,	I you he she it we you they	can't. shouldn't.	

Information questions

Who What	can should	I you	see?
When Why How	can should	he she it	help?
Where	can should	we you they	travel?

THERE IS/THERE ARE

Statements		
There	is	a pencil.
	are	pencils.

Negative statements		
There	isn't	a pencil.
	aren't	pencils.

Yes/No questions		
Is	there	a pencil.
Are		pens?

Answers					
Yes,	there	is.	No,	there	isn't.
		are.			aren't.

Questions with How many			
How many	pens	are	there?

Answers		
There	is	one pen.
	are	two pens.

THIS, THAT, THESE, AND THOSE

Singular statements		Notes
This That	couch is new.	Use *this* and *these* when the people or things are near.
This That	is new.	

Plural statements		Notes
These Those	couches are new.	Use *that* and *those* when the people or things are far.
These Those	are new.	

Yes/No questions	Answers
Is that couch new?	Yes, it is.

Yes/No questions	Answers
Are these couches new?	Yes, they are.

A, AN, ANY, AND SOME

Singular questions		Answers
Do you have	a tomato? an onion?	Yes, I have an onion.
		No, I don't have an onion.

Plural questions			Answers
Do you have	any	tomatoes? onions?	Yes, I have some tomatoes.
			No, I don't have any tomatoes.

NOUNS

To make plural nouns	Examples	
For most nouns, add -s.	chair—chairs	office—offices
If nouns end in -s, -z, -sh, -ch, -x, add -es.	bus—buses	lunch—lunches
If nouns end in consonant + -y, change -y to -ies.	family—families	factory—factories
If nouns end in vowel + -y, keep -y.	boy—boys	day—days
For most nouns that end in -o, add -s.	photo—photos	radio—radios
For some nouns that end in -o, add -es.	tomato—tomatoes	potato—potatoes
For most nouns that end in -f or -fe, change -f or -fe to v. Add -es.	wife—wives	half—halves
Some plural nouns do not end in -s, -es, or -ies. They are irregular plurals.	child—children	person—people

PRONOUNS AND POSSESSIVE ADJECTIVES

Subject pronouns	Object pronouns	Possessive adjectives
I	me	my
you	you	your
he	him	his
she	her	her
it	it	its
we	us	our
you	you	your
they	them	their

POSSESSIVES

Singular nouns		Notes
Tom's The manager's The factory's The woman's The person's	office is big.	Use -'s after a name, person, or thing for the possessive. Tom's the factory's

Plural regular nouns		Notes
The managers' The factories'	offices are big.	For plural nouns, change -s to -s'. the managers'

Plural irregular nouns		Notes
The women's The people's	office is big.	For irregular plurals, add -'s. women's

Information questions		
What colour is	my your Tom's Sara's the cat's our your their	hair?

Answers	
My Your His Her Its Our Your Their	hair is black.

PREPOSITIONS

Times and dates		Notes
The party is	on Tuesday. on June 16th.	Use *on* for days and dates.
The party is	at 9:30. at 9 o'clock.	Use *at* for times.

Locations		
The bank is	next to behind in front of across from	the library.
The bank is	between	the library and the store.

FREQUENCY AND TIME EXPRESSIONS

Frequency expressions			
I You	exercise		
He She It	exercises	every once a twice a three times a	day. week. month. year.
We You They	exercise		

Adverbs of frequency		
I You		exercise.
He She It	always usually sometimes	exercises.
We You They	never	exercise.

Questions and answers with *How often*	
A: How often do they exercise? B: They exercise every month.	A: How often does she exercise? B: She always exercises.
A: How often does he exercise? B: He exercises once a day.	A: How often do you exercise? B: I never exercise.

STATEMENTS WITH *AND, BUT, OR*

Notes	Examples
To combine sentences, use *and*. Change the first period to a comma.	I need a quarter. Amy wants a dime. I need a quarter, and Amy wants a dime.
For sentences with different ideas, use *but*. Change the first period to a comma.	I have a nickel. I don't have a quarter. I have nickel, but I don't have a quarter.
To combine two options, use *or*. Change the first period to a comma.	I want 10¢. I need a dime. I need ten pennies. I want 10¢. I need a dime, or I need ten pennies.

VOCABULARY LIST

Plans, 139, 141, 147
Preventive care, 108, 109
Prices, 77, 82, 83
Restaurant, ordering food, 94, 95
Road safety, 125, 132
Safety checklist, 127
Schedules, 65, 67
Shopping and money, 85
Talking about clothes, 79–81, 87
Things in the home, 41, 43
Time, 17
Utility bills, 46, 48, 49
Work safety, 125, 136

Writing

Addressing envelopes, 49
Calendar words, 17, 27
Classroom directions, 5
Classrooms, 9, 15
Clothing, 77, 81
Daily routines, 65, 68, 69, 71–73, 75
Describing people, 30–33, 38, 39
Doctor's appointments, 102, 107
Employment, 112–117, 123
Food, 91
Food labels, 97
Food shopping, 91, 93
Giving advice, 147
Grocery shopping, 91, 93
Illnesses and injuries, 111
Interpersonal information, 18, 21, 25, 27
Leisure Activities, 137, 139
Medicine labels, 109
Menu prices, 94
Money, 76, 77, 83
Neighborhood places, 52, 53, 55–57, 59, 62, 63
Numbers, 35, 46, 47, 83
Obligations, 105, 107, 111
Office machines and equipment, 70
Parts of the body, 100, 101
Places and activities in the home, 40, 43, 45, 51
Plans, 139, 141, 147
Restaurant, ordering food, 95
Road safety, 125, 135
Safe and unsafe behavior, 126, 127
Safety equipment, 125
Schedules, 67, 69
Shopping, 79
Things in the home, 43, 51
Time cards, 121
Transportation, 53
Utility bills, 46, 48, 49

CIVICS

Directory (Locate maps and services), 52–55, 58, 59, 61
Diversity, 18, 19, 21, 24–27
Emergencies, 130–132, 134

Employment requirements, 112, 113, 116–119, 122
Employment resources, 114, 115, 123
Employment safety, 125, 127, 135
Health care, 101–103, 106–110
Health—emergencies, 129–131, 134
Locating community resources, 46, 49, 145
Nutrition, 96, 97, 99
Pharmacy, 109
Recreation, 137–143, 147
Safety measures, 124–129, 132, 133, 135

LIFE SKILLS

Consumer Education

ATMs and banking, 84, 85
Clothing, 77, 79, 82, 83
Counting and using currency, 76, 77, 83
Identifying clothing, 77–79
Restaurant menus, 94, 95
Selecting clothing, 82
Utility bills, 46–49

Environment and the World

Maps, 59
Weather, 136, 137, 146, 147

Family and Parenting

Family members, 28–30, 32, 33, 38, 39
Family size, 36, 37
Holidays, 136

Government and Community Resources

Addresses, 6, 7, 49

Health and Nutrition

Body parts, 100, 101
Common illnesses and injuries, 101, 102
Directions and warnings on medicine labels, 109
Getting well and staying healthy, 103, 108
Healthy foods, 96, 97
Making a doctor's appointment, 106

Interpersonal Communication

Information about classmates, 25
Introductions, 10, 11, 15
Leisure activities, 137, 138, 142
Making plans, 139, 141, 147
Personal information, 7, 18
Personal interviews, 21, 27

Safety and Security

Emergencies, 130, 131
Home emergencies, 60, 61
Road safety, 125–127, 132, 135
Safe and dangerous behaviours, 126, 127
Safety checklists, 127
Work safety, 125, 135

TOPICS

WORKFORCE SKILLS

Applied Technology

Maintaining Employment

Obtaining Employment

ACKNOWLEDGEMENTS

Oxford University Press Canada and Sharon Rajabi would like to acknowledge the following individuals for their invaluable input during the development of this series:

Charles Austin Immigrant Services Society of BC, Vancouver, British Columbia

Vera Dickau Norquest College, Edmonton, Alberta

Susan Ellis Queen Elizabeth Secondary School, White Rock, British Columbia

Lisa Herrera Immigrant Services Society of BC, Vancouver, British Columbia

Joanne Hincks Toronto Catholic District School Board, Toronto, Ontario

Jane Kelly Chinook Learning Services, Calgary, Alberta

Aaron Kilner S.U.C.C.E.S.S., Burnaby, British Columbia

Beverly Knox St. Rita Catholic School, Toronto, Ontario

Daniel L. Love Calgary Immigrant Aid Society, Calgary, Alberta

Sylvia McCorkindale Saskatoon Open Door Society, Hepburn, Saskatchewan

Kata Niksic Vancouver Community College, Vancouver, British Columbia

Yasmin Ojah Saint John YM-YWCA, Saint John, New Brunswick

Beverley Payne Wheable Centre for Adult Education, London, Ontario

Shirene Salamatian Immigrant Services Society of BC, Vancouver, British Columbia

Ann Tigchelaar St. Vital Adult EAL Program, East Selkirk, Manitoba

Antonella Valeo Toronto Catholic District School Board, Toronto, Ontario

Terry Webb Wheable Centre for Adult Education, London, Ontario

Michelle Wong Immigrant Services Society of BC, Vancouver, British Columbia

---

The Publisher and Series Director would like to acknowledge the following individuals for their invaluable input during the development of this series:

Vittoria Abbatte-Maghsoudi Mount Diablo Unified School District, Loma Vista Adult Center, Concord, CA

Karen Abell Durham Technical Community College, Durham, NC

Millicent Alexander Los Angeles Unified School District, Huntington Park-Bell Community Adult School, Los Angeles, CA

Diana Allen Oakton Community College, Skokie, IL

Bethany Bandera Arlington Education and Employment Program, Arlington, VA

Sandra Bergman New York City Department of Education, New York, NY

Chan Bostwick Los Angeles Technology Center, Los Angeles, CA

Diana Brady-Herndon Napa Valley Adult School, Napa, CA

Susan Burlos Baldwin Park Unified School District, Baldwin Park, CA

Carmen Carbajal Mitchell Community College, Statesville, NC

Jose Carmona Daytona Beach Community College, Daytona Beach, FL

Ingrid Caswell Los Angeles Technology Center, Los Angeles, CA

Joyce Clapp Hayward Adult School, Hayward, CA **Beverly deNicola Capistrano** Unified School District, San Juan Capistrano, CA

Edward Ende Miami Springs Adult Center, Miami Springs, FL

Gayle Fagan Harris County Department of Education, Houston, TX

Richard Firsten Lindsey Hopkins Technical Education Center, Miami, FL

Elizabeth Fitzgerald Hialeah Adult Center, Hialeah, FL

Mary Ann Florez Arlington Education and Employment Program, Arlington, VA

Leslie Foster Davidson Mitchell Community College, Statesville, NC

Beverly Gandall Santa Ana College School of Continuing Education, Santa Ana, CA

Rodriguez Garner Westchester Community College, Valhalla, NY

Sally Gearhart Santa Rosa Junior College, Santa Rosa, CA

Norma Guzman Baldwin Park Unified School District, Baldwin Park, CA

Lori Howard UC Berkeley, Education Extension, Berkeley, CA

Phillip L. Johnson Santa Ana College Centennial Education Center, Santa Ana, CA

Kelley Keith Mount Diablo Unified School District, Loma Vista Adult Center, Concord, CA

Blanche Kellawon Bronx Community College, Bronx, NY

Keiko Kimura Triton College, River Grove, IL

Jody Kirkwood ABC Adult School, Cerritos, CA

Matthew Kogan Evans Community Adult School, Los Angeles, CA

Laurel Leonard Napa Valley Adult School, Napa, CA

Barbara Linek Illinois Migrant Education Council, Plainfield, IL

Alice Macondray Neighborhood Centers Adult School, Oakland, CA

Ronna Magy Los Angeles Unified School District Central Office, Los Angeles, CA

Jose Marlasca South Area Adult Education, Melbourne, FL

Laura Martin Adult Learning Resource Center, Des Plaines, IL

Judith Martin-Hall Indian River Community College, Fort Pierce, FL

Michael Mason Mount Diablo Unified School District, Loma Vista Adult Center, Concord, CA

Katherine McCaffery Brewster Technical Center, Tampa, FL

Cathleen McCargo Arlington Education and Employment Program, Arlington, VA

Todd McDonald Hillsborough County Public Schools, Tampa, FL

Rita McSorley Northeast Independent School District, San Antonio, TX

Gloria Melendrez Evans Community Adult School, Los Angeles, CA

Vicki Moore El Monte-Rosemead Adult School, El Monte, CA

Meg Morris Mountain View Los Altos Adult Education District, Los Altos, CA

Nieves Novoa LaGuardia Community College, Long Island City, NY

Jo Pamment Haslett Public Schools, East Lansing, MI

Liliana Quijada-Black Irvington Learning Center, Houston, TX

Ellen Quish LaGuardia Community College, Long Island City, NY

Mary Ray Fairfax County Public Schools, Springfield, VA

Tatiana Roganova Hayward Adult School, Hayward, CA

Nancy Rogenscky-Roda Hialeah-Miami Lakes Adult Education and Community Center, Hialeah, FL

Lorraine Romero Houston Community College, Houston, TX

Edilyn Samways The English Center, Miami, FL

Kathy Santopietro Weddel Northern Colorado Literacy Program, Littleton, CO

Dr. G. Santos The English Center, Miami, FL

Fran Schnall City College of New York Literacy Program, New York, NY

Mary Segovia El Monte-Rosemead Adult School, El Monte, CA

Edith Smith City College of San Francisco, San Francisco, CA

Alisa Takeuchi Chapman Education Center Garden Grove, CA

Leslie Weaver Fairfax County Public Schools, Falls Church, VA

David Wexler Napa Valley Adult School, Napa, CA

Bartley P. Wilson Northeast Independent School District, San Antonio, TX

Emily Wonson Hunter College, New York, NY

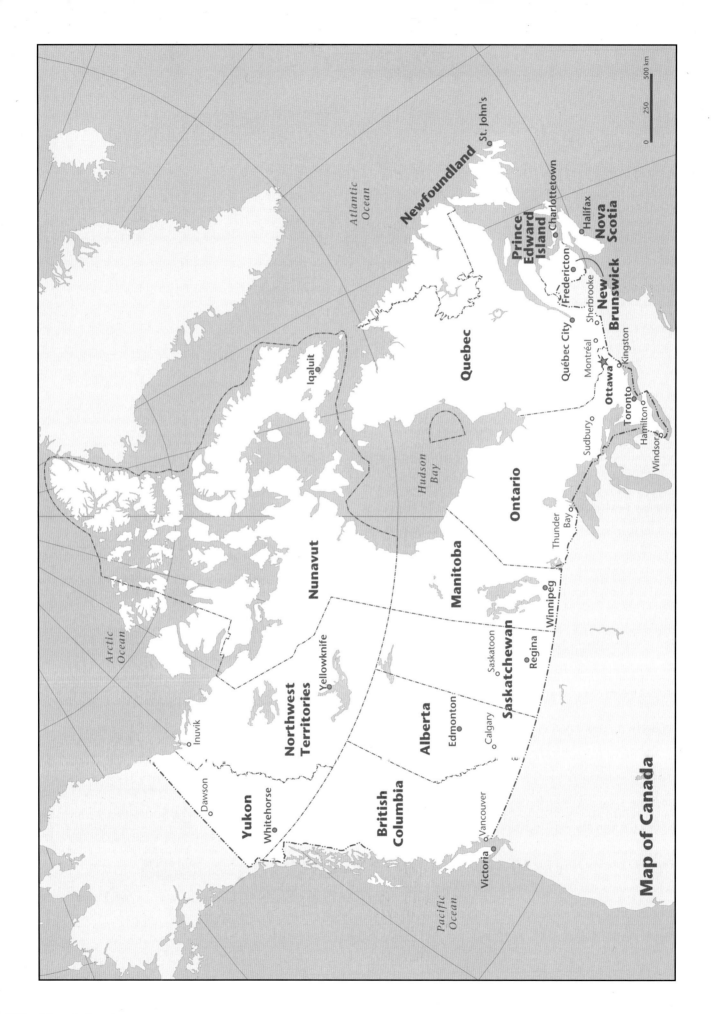

Map of Canada